Freedom of Expression

Freedom of Expression

Archibald Cox

Harvard University Press
Cambridge, Massachusetts
and London, England
1981

Freedom of Expression first appeared in
the *Harvard Law Review*, November 1980.

Library of Congress Cataloging in Publication Data
Cox, Archibald, 1912–
    Freedom of expression.
    1. Liberty of conscience — United States — Cases.
    2. Liberty of speech — United States — Cases.
    3. Liberty of the press — United States — Cases.
    I. Title.
    KF4770.A7C69 1981   342.73'0853'0264   81-4374
    ISBN 0-674-31912-5   347.3028530264   AACR2
    ISBN 0-674-31913-3 (pbk.)

CONTENTS

INTRODUCTION

Congress shall make no law respecting an establishment of religion, or prohibiting the free exercise thereof; or abridging the freedom of speech, or of the press; or the right of the people peaceably to assemble, and to petition the government for a redress of grievances.

S O reads the first article of amendment to the United States Constitution — the first in our Bill of Rights. The numerical position is symbolic because freedom of conscience and expression enjoys primacy in our scale of rights.

The juxtaposition of the key phrases in the first amendment reveals much of the philosophy underpinning those guarantees of particular fundamental rights. The framers put freedom of conscience first, and then moved on to freedom of speech and the press. They were concerned above all else with spiritual liberty: freedom to think, to believe, and to worship. They knew also that a man burdened with an idea has a need, even feels a moral duty, to express it. The thinking man or woman, the man or woman of feeling, the novelist, the poet or dramatist, the artist, and especially the evangelist can experience no greater affront to their humanity than denial of freedom of expression. It was natural, therefore, to move in sequence from freedom of conscience to freedom of speech and only then to freedom of the press.

Liberty of expression benefits more than the speaker. The hearer and reader suffer a violation of their spiritual liberty if they are denied access to the ideas of others.[1] When first considered, freedom of speech and the press chiefly meant opportunity to hear and read the word of God and thus to discover the road to salvation.

Perhaps it is only to restate these thoughts in somewhat different words to suggest that the second ground for assigning primacy to freedom of expression, and of access to ideas and knowledge, is that the liberty is essential to the pursuit of

---

[1] For a contemporary discussion of the importance of expression to the reader's or listener's autonomy, see Scanlon, *A Theory of Freedom of Expression*, 1 PHILOSOPHY & PUB. AFF. 204 (1972).

truth. Thomas Jefferson, James Madison, and the other Founding Fathers were children of the Enlightenment. They believed above all else in the power of reason, in the search for truth, in progress and the ultimate perfectibility of man. Freedom of inquiry and liberty of expression were deemed essential to the discovery and spread of truth, for only by the endless testing of debate could error be exposed, truth emerge, and men enjoy the opportunities for human progress.[2]

After John Stuart Mill we should perhaps speak only of the ability to progress *towards truth*, and of the value of the process of searching. The complete liberal posits that he has not reached, and probably could never reach, the ultimate truth. He hopes by constant search — by constant open debate, by trial and error — to do a little better; meanwhile he supposes that the process of searching has inestimable value because the lessons of the search — the readiness to learn, the striving to understand the minds and hearts and needs of other men, the effort to weigh their interests with his own — exemplify the only foundation upon which men can live and grow together.

The authors of the first amendment moved from religious liberty through the freedoms of speech and the press to the political rights to assemble peaceably and to petition government for the redress of grievances. Thus, as the freedoms of speech and of the press are linked to spiritual liberty on the one side, so they are tied to and find justification in political liberty and democracy on the other.

For some years now the tendency in the United States has been to emphasize the political aspect of freedom of speech. Alexander Meiklejohn, perhaps the foremost American philosopher of freedom of expression, was even willing to concede that the scholar's freedom to pursue knowledge may be abridged because knowledge may bring irretrievable disaster to mankind, but with respect to speech upon issues with which

---

[2] The 1979 controversy over the issue of *The Progressive* purporting to disclose the secret of hydrogen bomb design illustrates this aspect of the privilege of freedom of speech. *See* United States v. Progressive, Inc., 467 F. Supp. 990 (W.D. Wis.), *appeal dismissed*, 610 F.2d 819 (7th Cir. 1979), *summarized at* note 10 *infra*.

voters have to deal, his views were absolute. Whereas other constitutional guarantees are restrictions protecting the citizens against abuse of the powers delegated to government, Dr. Meiklejohn contended, the guarantees of freedom of speech and of the press hold an absolute, preferred position because they are measures adopted by the people as the ultimate rulers in order to retain control over government, the people's legislative and executive agents.[3] James Madison, the author of the first amendment, expressed a similar thought when he wrote, "If we advert to the nature of Republican Government, we shall find that the censorial power is in the people over the Government, and not in the Government over the people."[4] Only by uninhibited publication can the flow of information be secured and the people informed concerning men, measures, and the conduct of government. Only by freedom of expression can the people voice their grievances and obtain redress. Only by speech and the press can they exercise the power of criticism. Only by freedom of speech, of the press, and of association can people build and assert political power, including the power to change the men who govern them.

The political foundations of the first amendment are often emphasized in the opinions of the Supreme Court of the United States. In *Garrison v. Louisiana*,[5] Justice Brennan explained: "[S]peech concerning public affairs is more than self-expression; it is the essence of self-government."[6] Justice Harlan's thoughtful and eloquent opinion for the Court in *Cohen v. California*[7] is one of the few statements to reach for a deeper philosophic chord:

> The constitutional right of free expression . . . is designed and intended to remove governmental restraints from the arena of public discussion, putting the decision as to what views shall be voiced largely into the hands of each of us, in the hope

---

[3] A. MEIKLEJOHN, FREE SPEECH AND ITS RELATION TO SELF-GOVERNMENT (1948).
[4] 4 ANNALS OF CONG. 934 (1794).
[5] 379 U.S. 64 (1964).
[6] *Id.* at 74–75.
[7] 403 U.S. 15 (1971).

that use of such freedom will ultimately produce a more capable citizenry and more perfect polity and in the belief that
no other approach would comport with the premise of individual dignity and choice upon which our political system
rests.[8]

Freedom of expression, despite its primacy, can never be
absolute. In times of war or similar crisis some publications
may threaten even the survival of the Nation. At any time
unrestrained expression may conflict with important public or
private interests. Defamatory publications may unfairly in-
vade the interest in reputation. Impugning the integrity of a
court by publishing evidence in advance of trial may endanger
the administration of justice. Obscenity may conflict with the
interest in public morality. Picketing, parades, other forms of
demonstration, and sometimes even words themselves, if permitted at a particular time and place, may threaten public
safety or order regardless of the information, the ideas, or the
emotions expressed.

Some balancing is inescapable. The ultimate question is
always, Where has — and should — the balance be struck?
Yet the way in which the Court goes about striking the balance
makes a difference. The American judge's traditional responsibility embraces an antinomy: he is to render a decision consistent with the maintenance of a coherent body of continuing
law as binding upon him as upon the litigants, yet he is also
to keep the body of law in tune with the contemporary needs
of an ever-changing society. No sources of law singularly or
all together substitute for wisdom, perception, moderation, and
responsibility in deciding a hard case. But attention to the
structure and coherence of the surrounding body of law as
each case is decided finds and provides guidance for both
immediate and future decisions, reduces their subjectivity, and
strengthens their claim to legitimacy and thus, to general ac-
ceptance.

It has been roughly a decade since the era of the Warren
Court yielded to the Court presided over by Chief Justice

---

[8] *Id.* at 24.

Burger. The major first amendment cases decided during the past Term thus furnish a convenient occasion to review the work of the Burger Court in terms not only of the balances struck but also of the performance of its responsibility for the body of law defining freedom of speech and of the press under the first amendment.[9]

I. REGULATION OF CONTENT

Laws restricting freedom of expression may be classified usefully according to their functions. Some laws may restrict access to particular information, ideas, or emotions upon the ground that dissemination of the message will do harm to public or private interests: for example, the disclosure of the sailing date of a troopship in time of war or a false and defamatory statement. Other laws may restrict expression at a particular time or place or in a particular manner because the actor's conduct (including speaking) at that time or place, or of that character, will do harm to public or private interests regardless of the message, as in the case of a politician who places his soapbox at the center of the intersection of Fifth Avenue and Forty-Second Street, New York, or a demonstrator who expresses his contempt for civil authority by punching a policeman. Still other laws may indirectly interfere with expression by curtailing opportunities or adding to expense, as in the case of the rationing of paper during a war or of the application of a minimum wage law to newspapers along with the generality of employers. Not infrequently the restriction may be based upon a combination of message and circumstances, as in the case of incitement to riot or of massed pickets

---

[9] For a different perspective, see Emerson, *First Amendment Doctrine and the Burger Court*, 68 CALIF. L. REV. 422 (1980).

Discussion of two significant areas of first amendment law is omitted: the law of obscenity and the law governing claims of access to media. Reference to the 14th amendment is also omitted. The first amendment has been held to be incorporated into the 14th amendment since Gitlow v. New York, 268 U.S. 652 (1925), and is thus applicable to the states.

around a courthouse demanding the conviction of an unpopular defendant.

Drawing such lines is often difficult. It often involves more judgment than verbal logic. Classification is important, however, because the earlier efforts to bring all first amendment cases under a "clear and present danger" test have rightly given way to a variety of standards keyed to the character of the restriction. Restrictions based upon the harm done by the message are hardest to justify, especially when the ideas or information relates to the conduct of public affairs.

A. Restrictions upon Ideas and Information Relating to Public Affairs

1. National Interests. — By the 1970's the prosecutions for words and political associations spawned by World War I, the "Red Scare" of the 1920's, and the Cold War of 1945–1960 had faded. The only major case presenting a direct conflict between first amendment freedoms and the national security as perceived by the Executive arose from the threatened publication of the so-called Pentagon Papers.[10]

The facts are familiar. Daniel Ellsberg made copies of highly secret, classified government papers reviewing the formulation of U.S. policy towards Indochina, including military

---

[10] New York Times Co. v. United States, 403 U.S. 713 (1971). Another dramatic and potentially important case developed in 1979 when the federal government learned that *The Progressive* magazine intended to publish an article entitled *The H-bomb Secret: How We Got It, Why We're Telling It*. The author purported to disclose in a form understandable to the layman previously secret technical material on the design of a hydrogen bomb. United States v. Progressive, Inc., 467 F. Supp. 990 (W.D. Wis.), *appeal dismissed*, 610 F.2d 819 (7th Cir. 1979). The Atomic Energy Act of 1954, 42 U.S.C. §§ 2011–2296 (1976), forbids the publication or disclosure of information that may be useful in the manufacture of nuclear weapons, *id.* § 2274(b), and also authorizes injunctive relief, *id.* § 2380. The district court issued an injunction forbidding the publication, but the suit lost significance and the government abandoned its pursuit of the injunction when it became plain that the information was already available in other publications. Although the defendants argued only the political importance of publication, the statutory prohibition might also be vulnerable to challenge under the first amendment as a barrier to the free pursuit of scientific knowledge.

operations and secret diplomatic negotiations. The papers had been entrusted to him in confidence while he did work for the government. He abstracted the copies and gave these abstracts and selected excerpts to newspapers for publication. The Executive rushed to the courts to enjoin publication, making strong representations that the risk of injury to national interests if the Pentagon Papers were published included the death of soldiers, the destruction of alliances, the greatly increased difficulty of negotiation with our enemies, the inability of our diplomats to negotiate, and the prolongation of the war.[11] The Court ruled that these claims would not support an injunction against publication, even for the period necessary to study how far the fears were justified. There was no opinion of the Court.

The individual opinions reveal marked differences of judicial style. Justices Black and Douglas declared that *ever* to permit any prior restraint upon the publication of any news would "make a shambles of the First Amendment."[12] Yet surely they would not have ruled during World War II that a newspaper had a constitutional right to publish for Nazi eyes the knowledge that, because of the cryptographic work at Bletchley, British authorities were reading the orders of the Nazi High Command.

Justice Brennan was slightly less enthusiastic but still vigorous in condemning prior restraints: "[O]nly governmental allegation and proof that publication must inevitably, directly, and immediately cause the occurrence of an event kindred to imperiling the safety of a transport already at sea can support even the issuance of an interim restraining order."[13] In this case, he concluded, the government had failed to show with sufficient certainty that publication would injure the national interest.

The other three Justices in the six-man majority — Stewart, White, and Marshall — put less weight upon the first

---

[11] *See also* 403 U.S. at 762–63 (Blackmun, J., dissenting).
[12] *Id.* at 715 (Black, J., concurring).
[13] *Id.* at 726–27 (Brennan, J., concurring).

amendment than upon the absence of statutory authority for
the issuance of an injunction. In the words of Justice White,
joined by Justice Stewart, "At least in the absence of legislation
by Congress, based on its own investigations and findings, I
am quite unable to agree that the inherent powers of the
Executive and the courts reach so far as to authorize remedies
having such sweeping potential for inhibiting publications by
the press."[14] Justice Stewart, in an opinion joined by Justice
White, apparently reserved some room for a judicially imposed
restraint even in the absence of a statute, for he observed that
there was only one possible answer to the questions before the
Court in the absence of proof that disclosure would "surely
result in direct, immediate, and irreparable damage to our
Nation or its people."[15] Justice Marshall was of the view that
no injunction should issue because Congress had considered
and refused to enact appropriate legislation.[16] Because there
were three dissenters and Justices Black and Douglas have left
the Court, it seems unlikely that the Court would now refuse
an injunction when the government submitted proof adequate
to satisfy the necessarily somewhat vague test stated by Justices Stewart and White.

The Case of the Pentagon Papers left other questions unanswered. (1) Would the first amendment have permitted an
injunction if Congress had enacted the necessary statutory

---

[14] *Id.* at 732 (White, J., concurring).

[15] *Id.* at 730 (Stewart, J., concurring). Justice Stewart's opinion also contains a
puzzling assertion that "[i]t is the constitutional duty of the Executive — as a matter
of sovereign prerogative and not as a matter of law as the courts know law — through
the promulgation and enforcement of Executive regulations, to protect the confidentiality necessary to carry out its responsibilities in the fields of international relations
and national defense." *Id.* at 729–30. Earlier in the same paragraph Justice Stewart
had declared that "[t]he responsibility must be where the power is." *Id.* at 728.
Probably this passage asserts no more than that the initial steps must be taken by
executive order, or that in the absence of legislation the executive must rely upon
disciplinary power over employees who violate security regulations. The passage can
be read, however, to imply the rather startling assertion that the Executive should
have used its "sovereign prerogative" if it wished to prevent the *New York Times*
from publishing the Pentagon Papers.

[16] *Id.* at 740–48 (Marshall, J., concurring).

authority? (2) Would the first amendment have permitted prosecution of either Ellsberg or the New York Times and Washington Post if a statute had prohibited their conduct?[17] (3) If the government had learned of Ellsberg's intention to give copies of the Pentagon Papers to the newspapers, might the government have secured an injunction against the distribution? (4) Might the government have obtained an injunction against the newspapers upon alleging and proving that they were, in fact, receivers of stolen goods because they received the photocopies knowing them to have been made and released by Ellsberg in breach of confidence?

Last Term's decision in *Snepp v. United States*[18] throws a little light upon the answers to the third and fourth questions. Frank W. Snepp, III became an agent of the Central Intelligence Agency (CIA) in 1968 upon executing an agreement that he would not "publish . . . any information or material relating to the Agency, its activities or intelligence activities generally, either during or after the term of [his] employment . . . without specific prior approval by the Agency."[19] Snepp deliberately and surreptitiously published an account of CIA activities in South Vietnam under the title *Decent Interval*, without submitting the manuscript to the CIA for prior approval. Thereafter the United States brought an action seeking (1) a declaration that Snepp had violated the contract, (2) an injunction requiring Snepp to submit future writings for prepublication review, and (3) an order imposing a constructive trust for the benefit of the United States on any profits that Snepp had received from the publication of *Decent Interval*. It was stipulated that *Decent Interval* contained no classified information.

The district court granted the relief requested.[20] The Court of Appeals for the Fourth Circuit modified the judgment to

---

[17] The question would have been presented had the *Progressive* case reached the Supreme Court.

[18] 444 U.S. 507 (1980) (per curiam).

[19] *Id.* at 508.

[20] United States v. Snepp, 456 F. Supp. 176 (E.D. Va. 1978).

deny the imposition of a constructive trust.[21] On Snepp's
petition for certiorari, and the United States' conditional cross-
petition, the Supreme Court in a per curiam opinion summarily
affirmed the portions of the judgment adverse to Snepp and
reversed the portion of the judgment adverse to the United
States without affording opportunity for full briefs and oral
argument. Three Justices dissented.[22]

It is hardly surprising that Snepp's conduct aroused the
scorn of a majority of the Justices even though the use of the
"leak" as an instrument of political conflict and its sanctifica-
tion by the mass media have unfortunately dulled some moral
sensibilities. The political impact of Ellsberg's release of the
Pentagon Papers has led too many to conclude too easily that
in this area the end justifies the means. On the facts found
below, Snepp's publication of *Decent Interval* was not merely
the deliberate breach of a binding contract but a shabby violation of a personal confidence voluntarily accepted.

But judicial indignation, even when justified, is not an
acceptable substitute for a full hearing and a reasoned opinion.
The summary disposition denied Snepp's attorneys the opportunity to brief and to argue orally a number of important
points bearing upon both the enforceability of the contract and
the appropriateness of the remedy.[23] The summary opinion
evades the difficulties.

The per curiam opinion upholds the agreement in a footnote as "a reasonable means for protecting" the "secrecy of
information important to our national security and the ap-
pearance of confidentiality so essential to the effective opera-

---

[21] United States v. Snepp, 595 F.2d 926 (4th Cir. 1979).

[22] Justice Stevens filed a dissenting opinion in which Justices Brennan and Marshall joined. 444 U.S. at 516–26.

[23] Even though the situations are distinguishable, the majority's abrupt disposition
of the *Snepp* case with the Chief Justice's leadership or concurrence contrasts with
the Chief Justice's dissenting protest against the "frenetic haste" with which the Court
dissolved the prior restraint upon speech after an accelerated schedule of briefs and
argument in the case of the Pentagon Papers. *See* New York Times Co. v. United
States, 403 U.S. 713, 748–52 (1971) (Burger, C.J., dissenting).

tion of our foreign intelligence service."[24] Perhaps so; nay, probably so. But it is certainly arguable, as Justice Stevens pointed out in dissent,[25] that the contract subjected Snepp's right to criticize the government to an excessively severe and time-consuming prior restraint by requiring CIA clearance of any book or article that Snepp might write, even one containing absolutely no classified information. CIA censorship appears to have gone beyond matters relevant to security.[26] The pressure to trim in order to satisfy the censor is ever present. It is not enough to say that Snepp's entirely voluntary undertaking should operate as a waiver of his constitutional rights.

In the end, the question may be of the citizenry's right to know about the conduct of its government. In a variety of contexts in which there were plausible arguments to uphold the particular regulation of a speaker against challenge under the first amendment the Court has turned the argument by stressing the role of the amendment "in affording the public access to discussion, debate, and the dissemination of information and ideas."[27] One would have supposed that the extent of the government's authority to silence its officials and employees and thereby deprive the public of access to information about government activity was not too obvious to deserve deliberate judicial consideration.

A coincidence made full briefs and argument even more appropriate. When *Snepp* was so summarily decided, the Court had under consideration *Richmond Newspapers, Inc. v. Virginia*,[28] where some of the Justices — a majority according to Justice Stevens[29] — later held that the first amendment gives not only a right to publish but, at least under some

[24] Snepp v. United States, 444 U.S. 507, 509 n.3 (1980).

[25] *Id.* at 519, 526 (Stevens, J., dissenting).

[26] Lewis, *Mind of the Censor*, N.Y. Times, Apr. 7, 1980, at A19, col. 1.

[27] First Nat'l Bank v. Bellotti, 435 U.S. 765, 783 (1978). *See also* Red Lion Broadcasting Co. v. FCC, 395 U.S. 367, 389–90 (1969); Lamont v. Postmaster Gen., 381 U.S. 301 (1965).

[28] 100 S. Ct. 2814 (1980); *see* pp. 24–32 *infra*.

[29] 100 S. Ct. at 2831 (Stevens, J., concurring).

circumstances, a right to acquire for publication ideas and information pertaining to the conduct of government. Because none of the material in Snepp's book was classified, members of the public, including Snepp's publisher, also arguably had a statutory right to the material under the Freedom of Information Act.[30] Perhaps these rights must be subordinated to the interest of the government in gaining — and in giving allies of the United States — assurance that proper security is not violated by a book written by a CIA employee with access to classified information. The question was novel, however, and the answer is not so obvious that an openminded bench could not benefit from argument, if not in reaching a conclusion then in providing reasoned elaboration fitting the decision into the relevant body of law. The opinion rests enforcement of the contract upon bare assertion without mention of the competing public interests. The failure to receive briefs and argument on the merits, coupled with the inadequate, summary opinion in a sensitive area, serves chiefly to arouse the critics of secrecy; it also lessens confidence in the Court.[31]

The summary treatment accorded Snepp takes one back to the questions concerning the extent of the constitutional privilege of a publisher who receives documents such as the Pen-

---

[30] 5 U.S.C. § 552 (1976).

[31] The summary imposition of a constructive trust upon Snepp's royalties seems subject to similar criticism. Serious difficulties are buried within the bland statement that "since the remedy reaches only funds attributable to the breach, it cannot saddle the former agent with exemplary damages out of all proportion to his gain." Snepp v. United States, 444 U.S. 507, 515–16 (1980). Snepp's profits were derived from publication of the book. Snepp had a right to publish the book, after CIA clearance. Because the book contained no classified information, the CIA had a duty to clear the book. To assert without explanation that Snepp's profits were "attributable" to the omission of this formality is an oversimplification, to say the least. Possibly, Snepp should be deprived of his profits without regard to problems of causation. Possibly, Snepp, as a wrongdoer, should bear the burden of disentangling the profits, if any, flowing from the wrong from the profits that he alleges that he would have received if he had sought the clearance to which he was entitled. All these issues were novel, however, and a majority of the court of appeals had thought the remedy inappropriate. Three Justices expressed doubt. Under these circumstances, reversal on the merits without argument seems hardly consonant with due deliberation.

tagon Papers or a manuscript such as that Snepp submitted in breach of his agreement. The publisher might be entirely ignorant of the violation; it might have notice but not knowledge; or it might have actively induced the breach of contract. Because *Decent Interval* contained no classified material, the rejection of Snepp's first amendment defense must have been based partly upon the reprehensible character of his conduct and the need to deter such conduct in the future, rather than upon a simple balancing of the gains and costs of the release of the particular ideas and information. Might not a publisher likewise be charged with participation in the wrong? The argument would be strongest when the publisher induced the violation; weaker when the publisher was a passive recipient; and probably untenable in the unlikely event that the publisher had no notice of the agreement.

The closest precedent upon the questions is *Landmark Communications, Inc. v. Virginia*.[32] There a unanimous bench set aside the conviction of a newspaper publisher for accurately reporting the status of an inquiry pending before the Virginia Judicial Inquiry and Review Commission, in violation of a statute declaring that all such proceedings "shall be confidential and shall not be divulged by any person to anyone except the Commission."[33] The Chief Justice's opinion for the Court reasoned that the decision was controlled by prior cases reversing convictions for contempt of court based upon criticism of the decisions or conduct of judges in public judicial proceedings; the state, he said, had failed to prove that the publication gave rise to a clear and present danger of interference with the administration of justice.[34] The opinion ignored the seemingly material difference between publishing information or commentary upon official business conducted in public and publicizing information that the state has rightfully sought to keep confidential and that has received even limited disclosure only by a criminal act. Similarly, the Chief Justice failed to

---

[32] 435 U.S. 829 (1978).
[33] VA. CODE § 2.1-37.13 (1973).
[34] 435 U.S. at 844–45.

explain why the state may punish the individual who reveals the confidential information to the press but not the publisher who causes the real harm by publicizing what it has been unlawfully told.[35]

Presumably the reason for the holding is that requiring a newspaper to decide at its peril whether information that it has received about an official proceeding is confidential would have a chilling effect upon the publication of legitimate news. It would be even more burdensome to impose a duty to inquire into the ultimate source of information and the conduct of the informant. The result is also consistent with the Burger Court's great sensitivity in other contexts to the claims of the press to be free from interference with the publication of any information that comes to its attention.[36] The same considerations would support extension of the *Landmark Communications* rule to situations involving national security. The arguments are somewhat weaker, however, and perhaps an exception might be made for instances in which the publisher has knowingly and actively induced the breach of confidence.

2. *Individual Reputation.* — In 1964 the Warren Court, sweeping aside 175 years of settled law, held in *New York Times Co. v. Sullivan*[37] that the first amendment bars a state from awarding a public official damages for a defamatory falsehood relating to his official conduct unless the falsehood is published with knowledge of its falsity or with reckless disregard for whether it is true or false. The theme is obviously libertarian and egalitarian. The opinion throbs with

---

[35] Justice Stewart's brief concurring opinion was more direct but no more explanatory: "[G]overnment may not prohibit or punish publication of that information once it falls into the hands of the press, unless the need for secrecy is manifestly overwhelming." *Id.* at 849.

[36] *See* pp. 19–24 *infra*. Note also that in Nebraska Press Ass'n v. Stuart, 427 U.S. 539, 572, 588 (1976), Justice Brennan, concurring, wrote:

> Settled case law concerning the impropriety and constitutional invalidity of prior restraints on the press compels the conclusion that there can be no prohibition on the publication by the press of any information pertaining to pending judicial proceedings or the operation of the criminal justice system, no matter how shabby the means by which the information is obtained.

[37] 376 U.S. 254 (1964).

faith in popular self-government resting upon the widest freedom of discussion. The holding enables the press to pursue investigations into corruption and other abuses of public position by relieving newspaper reporters, editors, and publishers of the worry that they might have to pay damages to a public person whom they injure by publishing what some jury later finds to be a false and defamatory statement of fact.

Later decisions extended the immunity to libels upon senior civil servants,[38] candidates for public office,[39] football coaches at state universities,[40] and sundry other public figures.[41] In 1971, in *Rosenbloom v. Metromedia, Inc.*,[42] a splintered Court applied the *New York Times* rule to defamation of a previously unknown private person. The plurality opinion would have extended the rule to any publication upon any matter of public interest, but the eight Justices who participated wrote five opinions, each of which advocated a different rule.[43] Working out limitations upon the *New York Times* immunity was thus left to the future.

The lines drawn have been less generous to the press than the press would wish; probably even a bit less generous than they ought to be. The enthusiasm of *New York Times v. Sullivan* has yielded to more cautious weighing and balancing based chiefly upon concern for the individual's interest in freedom from false exposure to public scandal. The decisions also may reflect a sense that putting some risk of liability upon the press when intruding into private lives will make for more responsible reporting without inhibiting criticism of govern-

---

[38] Rosenblatt v. Baer, 383 U.S. 75 (1966).

[39] Monitor Patriot Co. v. Roy, 401 U.S. 265 (1971).

[40] Curtis Publishing Co. v. Butts, 388 U.S. 130 (1967).

[41] *See, e.g.*, Associated Press v. Walker, 388 U.S. 130 (1967) (retired army general).

[42] 403 U.S. 29 (1971).

[43] Three Justices (Justice Brennan, joined by Chief Justice Burger and Justice Blackmun) put the decision upon the ground that the statement concerned a charge of commercial pornography, which was a subject of public interest. *Id.* at 43. Justice Black held that the first amendment bars any award of damages for libel. *Id.* at 57. (Justice Douglas, who did not participate, also held this opinion.) Justice White joined these four on the ground that the statement pertained to police activities. *Id.* at 57–62.

ment or political debate. The Chief Justice and Justices White
and Rehnquist appear to favor even stricter limitation upon
the constitutional privilege in order to allow the states to develop the law of defamation outside the area of official conduct
and political debate, where the underlying interest in freedom
of expression is at its peak.[44]

The basic line of limitation around the *New York Times*
privilege was drawn in *Gertz v. Robert Welch, Inc.*[45] Gertz,
a Chicago lawyer, had represented the family of a man killed
by a Chicago policeman, who was later convicted of murder.
Gertz had belonged to organizations like the National Lawyers
Guild and had played very minor roles in community affairs.
Robert Welch, Inc., an organ of the John Birch Society, published an article purporting to expose a leftwing conspiracy
against the police in the course of which the author made false
and defamatory statements about Gertz. Gertz brought an
action in federal court and obtained a favorable verdict even
though there was proof of neither recklessness nor intent. The
district court then entered judgment for the defendant not-
withstanding the verdict.[46] The court of appeals affirmed.[47]

The opinion of the Supreme Court illustrates the degree to
which the law of defamation has been "constitutionalized,"
and therefore "nationalized." Justice Powell follows the tech-
nique of a common law jurist balancing opposing interests
without precedent to control him. He found the interests to
be the circulation of information and debate upon matters of
public significance, on the one side, and the individual's private personality — his dignity and worth — on the other. In

---

[44] *See, e.g.*, Gertz v. Robert Welch, Inc., 418 U.S. 323, 354–55 (1974) (Burger,
C.J., dissenting); *id.* at 369–404 (White, J., dissenting); Miami Herald Publishing Co.
v. Tornillo, 418 U.S. 241, 259–63 (1974) (White, J., concurring). The characterization
of Justice Rehnquist's view may be unwarranted. It rests upon inference from his
opinions giving narrow scope to the *New York Times* immunity, *e.g.*, Time, Inc. v.
Firestone, 424 U.S. 448 (1976), and his emphasis upon state interests in other contexts,
e.g., National League of Cities v. Usery, 426 U.S. 833 (1976); Rizzo v. Goode, 423
U.S. 362 (1976).

[45] 418 U.S. 323 (1974).

[46] 322 F. Supp. 997 (N.D. Ill. 1970).

[47] 471 F.2d 801 (7th Cir. 1972).

the case of a public figure, the Justice concluded, the imposition of liability for anything less than an intentional or reckless falsehood carries too much risk of self-censorship resulting in suppression of truth, but the balance is to be struck more favorably for a private person because a private person, unlike a public official or public figure, does not voluntarily expose himself to risk of falsehood and lacks opportunity to command attention for his reply. Accordingly, four rules emerged:

(1) The Constitution gives the press absolute freedom to publish statements about "public figures" that turn out to be false, unless the publisher knew they were false or recklessly disregarded warning of their untruth.

(2) The first amendment frees the press from liability to other persons when there is neither negligence nor more serious fault.

(3) Conversely, the states are free to impose liability for defamation of a private person if the publisher or broadcaster is at fault.

(4) Damages may be awarded to compensate for "actual injury," but punitive damages will not be allowed unless the statements were intentionally or recklessly false. "Actual injury" includes impairment of standing in the community, personal humiliation, and mental suffering. Injury must be proved, however; it cannot be presumed from the fact of publication.

Gertz was held not to be a public figure because he had achieved no "general fame or notoriety in the community," and did not seek to influence public opinion or otherwise "thrust himself into the vortex" of the particular controversy.[48]

The *Gertz* case seems fairly typical of the Burger Court. The bench was so badly splintered as to produce six opinions,[49] espousing at least four sharply different constitutional

---

[48] 418 U.S. at 352.

[49] Justices Stewart, Marshall, Blackmun, and Rehnquist joined in Justice Powell's opinion of the Court, but Justice Blackmun filed a separate concurrence explaining that he joined only so that there might be a majority for some rule. *Id.* at 353–54. The Chief Justice, Justice Douglas, Justice Brennan, and Justice White filed separate dissents.

rules. The enthusiasm that often characterized the majority opinions of the Warren Court has yielded to cautious analysis. The decision continues the trend in "constitutionalizing" and thus "nationalizing" bodies of law previously left to the states by requiring proof of fault and restricting the damages recoverable. The careful reader of the *Gertz* opinion will sense an effort to take account of the insistence of the Chief Justice and Justice White that due concern for the balance of the federal system requires leaving questions pertaining to liability to nonpublic figures to the states. The net effect of the decision, however, was to extend the first amendment a little further by freeing the media entirely from liability for defamation without fault.

The subsequent cases give grudging scope to the concept of "public figure,"[50] and, in my view, give the concept excessive significance. In *Hutchinson v. Proxmire*,[51] for example, it appeared that the plaintiff had received more than $500,000 in grants from federal agencies for studies of aggressive behavior — such as jaw clenching — in animals and humans. Senator William Proxmire, who had initiated the practice of making a "Golden Fleece of the Month Award" in an effort to publicize wasteful governmental spending, held the plaintiff up to ridicule in making his award for March 1975: "Dr. Hutchinson's studies should make the taxpayers as well as his monkeys grind their teeth. In fact, the good doctor has made a fortune from his monkeys and in the process made a monkey out of the American taxpayer."[52]

When the good doctor brought a federal suit against the good Senator to recover damages for the allegedly false and defamatory statements, the lower courts gave judgment for the Senator upon the ground that the plaintiff had failed to prove that the statement was made with knowledge that it was false or with reckless indifference as to whether it was true or false.

---

[50] Wolston v. Reader's Digest Ass'n, 443 U.S. 157 (1979); Hutchinson v. Proxmire, 443 U.S. 111 (1979); Time, Inc. v. Firestone, 424 U.S. 448 (1976).

[51] 443 U.S. 111 (1979).

[52] *Id.* at 116.

The Supreme Court reversed upon the ground that the *New York Times* rule was inapplicable because the plaintiff was not a public figure. Even the most severe critic of the decision would find it difficult to argue that Dr. Hutchinson was in fact a "public figure." Probably most observers would agree that an individual who accepts a grant from the government to finance research should not be held to open all aspects of his or her life to the full extent of the *New York Times* rule. Yet the merits of the grant were surely public business. The ruling will tend to chill public debate about official folly in making wasteful grants. There is the same interest in public criticism and debate about the wisdom of the research when the recipient is the plaintiff as there is when the plaintiff is the government official who approved the project. The *New York Times* rule should apply to all activities voluntarily undertaken by or for the government without regard to whether the plaintiff is a public or private figure, but the full privilege should not extend to other parts of a private figure's life.[53]

Often the present Court seems much too pragmatic and particularistic. In this instance, I think, it erred by excessive generalization.

3. Individual Privacy. — The public interest in open discussion and debate sometimes collides with an individual's interest in privacy, even when accurate reports are concerned. The potential is present in much official business but it extends to other activity.

Self-governance in the United States presupposes far more than knowledge and debate about the strictly official activities of various levels of government. . . . "Freedom of discussion, if it would fulfill its historic function in this nation, must

---

[53] The rule suggested above differs from the "matter of public interest" rule advocated by the plurality in Rosenbloom v. Metromedia, Inc., 403 U.S. 29 (1971), because it would apply only to discussion of the conduct of governmental business. The suggestion parallels Justice White's concurring opinion in the *Metromedia* case, *id.* at 57–62.

embrace all issues about which information is needed or appropriate to enable the members of society to cope with the exigencies of their period."[54]

All but one of the cases to come before the Burger Court have grown out of a newspaper's or broadcaster's publication of information contained in a public record. In *Cox Broadcasting Corp. v. Cohn*,[55] the Court held that the first amendment prevents the award of damages to a father distressed by the broadcast of information that his daughter had been the victim of rape. The information was derived from the official public record of the ensuing prosecution of the rapist. *Smith v. Daily Mail Publishing Co.*[56] reversed a state court conviction of a publisher for printing the name of a juvenile offender in patent violation of a state criminal statute. Here again the information was available in an open public record. In *Landmark Communications, Inc. v. Virginia*,[57] however, the information concerned a proceeding that the state sought to keep confidential. The Court nevertheless held that publication was privileged.

These cases should be read with *Nebraska Press Association v. Stuart*[58] and the Pentagon Papers case.[59] Taken together they leave little doubt that, except in cases involving imminent national military catastrophe, the Court will not permit previous restraints upon, or subsequent punishment for, publication in a mass medium of accurate information that the publisher has lawfully acquired.

4. Fair Administration of Justice. — English law has long punished as contempt of court publications tending to influence the disposition of matters sub judice.[60] In one aspect the rule

---

[54] Rosenbloom v. Metromedia, Inc., 403 U.S. 29, 41 (1971) (quoting Thornhill v. Alabama, 310 U.S. 88, 102 (1940)).

[55] 420 U.S. 469 (1975).

[56] 443 U.S. 97 (1979).

[57] 435 U.S. 829 (1978).

[58] 427 U.S. 539 (1976), *discussed at* pp. 21–23 *infra*.

[59] 403 U.S. 713 (1971), *discussed at* pp. 6–9 *supra*.

[60] Goodhart, *Newspapers and Contempt of Court in English Law*, 48 HARV. L.

prevents newspaper editorials from advocating one or another disposition of a pending case, such as a heavy sentence, or a generous award of damages. In another aspect the rule precludes the pretrial publication of information, such as a report of a confession, that might prejudice potential jurors.

A series of decisions beginning in 1941 made it plain that adherence to the first branch of the English rule violates the first amendment.[61] The opinions assert that judges are made of stuff too stern to be subject to such influences,[62] but it seems more likely that the Court determined that the value of free discussion of this aspect of government outweighs the cost in actual or apparent extrajudicial influence upon the administration of justice.

Questions concerning the power to forbid prejudicial pretrial publicity came to a head in the *Nebraska Press* case.[63] The gory slaughter of an entire family in a little community of 850 persons attracted sustained news coverage by local, regional, and national newspapers, and radio and television stations. Local tension was high until a suspect, Simants, made a confession, which was introduced at a preliminary hearing. The hearing was open to the public. A restrictive order was entered that, as the case came before the U.S. Supreme Court, prohibited reporting of the existence or nature of the confession introduced at the hearing, or of any other facts strongly implicating the accused.[64]

The Supreme Court unanimously set aside the order as a violation of the first amendment. There were two principal opinions. One is typical of the libertarian Justices of the

---

REV. 885 (1935). For an extraordinarily restrictive example, see Attorney-General v. Times Newspapers Ltd., [1974] A.C. 273.

[61] *E.g.*, Wood v. Georgia, 370 U.S. 375 (1962); Bridges v. California, 314 U.S. 252 (1941). In Cox v. Louisiana, 379 U.S. 559 (1965), however, the Court refused to apply the same doctrine to courthouse picketing upon the ground that the prohibitory statute was narrowly drawn and dealt with picketing rather than pure speech.

[62] Cox v. Louisiana, 379 U.S. 559, 565 (1965); Wood v. Georgia, 370 U.S. 375, 391 n.18 (1962); Bridges v. California, 314 U.S. 252, 273 (1941).

[63] Nebraska Press Ass'n v. Stuart, 427 U.S. 539 (1976).

[64] *Id.* at 545.

1960's. Justice Brennan, with whom Justices Stewart and Marshall concurred, argued for an absolute rule that resort to prior restraints on the freedom of the press is never a constitutionally permissible method for protecting the right to a fair trial.[65] Here — these Justices seemed to say — is a chance to lay down a "right" rule for the defense of liberty. Opportunity may not come again. Moreover, such a rule would guide the lower courts in an area in which any decision at nisi prius forbidding publication has irreparable consequences.

The majority opinion is more typical of the Burger Court. In a cautious vein Chief Justice Burger weighed (1) the nature and extent of the pretrial publicity, (2) the degree to which other measures might effectively secure a fair trial despite unrestrained publicity, and (3) the degree to which a gag order would obviate the risk that an impartial jury could not be assembled. The Court then concluded that "the heavy burden imposed as a condition to securing a prior restraint was not met."[66]

I would have thought the caution of the majority opinion amply justified by the difficulty of the problem and the limitations upon human foresight if the Chief Justice had more carefully confined the opinion to the case at hand. Instead, he went further to declare, "We reaffirm that the guarantees of freedom of expression are not an absolute prohibition under all circumstances . . . ."[67] The case did not require this pronouncement. Only a bare majority of the Justices concurred in it. A stronger case for a "gag order" is not likely to develop. Decisions in related fields indicate that the Court is now committed to a virtually absolute rule protecting the publication of any information concerning public affairs acquired by a reporter without violating the law.[68]

With the privilege to publish secured, the interest of the press in *access* to judicial proceedings intensified. The public-

---

[65] *Id.* at 572–613 (Brennan, J., concurring).
[66] 427 U.S. at 570.
[67] *Id.*
[68] *See* pp. 17–20 *supra*.

ity given to Simants' confession could have been avoided and the threat to the fairness of any subsequent trial could have been reduced by closing the preliminary hearing with Simants' consent — if permitted by state law and the Federal Constitution. This course was followed in a highly publicized murder prosecution in upstate New York when the defendant moved to suppress certain damaging evidence and asked that the pretrial hearing on the motion be closed. The Gannett newspapers then attacked the order barring the public and the press from the pretrial hearing, and carried the case to the Supreme Court of the United States.

The majority opinion rejected Gannett's sixth amendment argument for two reasons. First, the Court held that the words "the accused shall enjoy the right to a speedy and public trial" give no rights to the public or the press.[69] Second, the Court found that the words, "public trial" would not support the claim to public pretrial hearings.[70] Justice Blackmun's dissent demonstrated that a public right to open judicial proceedings was acknowledged and public trials were the custom at the time the Constitution was adopted,[71] but his reasoning fell short of demonstrating that the public right was to be secured by federal guarantee in the sixth amendment.

Gannett's first amendment claim raised broader and more difficult questions. In the past the privilege secured by the first amendment had been treated as a guarantee of freedom to publish such information as the press may obtain and such commentary or criticism as it may desire. A majority of the Justices had consistently rejected claims of a first amendment right of access to information about closed governmental activity.[72] To accept the argument in any form might well be thought to present the courts with the extraordinarily difficult, if not impossible, task of determining where to draw the line

---

[69] Gannett Co. v. DePasquale, 443 U.S. 368, 379–84 (1979).

[70] Id. at 384–91.

[71] Id. at 419–26 (Blackmun, J., dissenting).

[72] Houchins v. KQED, Inc., 438 U.S. 1, 8–16 (1978); Nixon v. Warner Communications, Inc., 435 U.S. 589, 608–10 (1978); Saxbe v. Washington Post Co., 417 U.S. 843, 850 (1974); Pell v. Procunier, 417 U.S. 817, 829–35 (1974).

between government proceedings to which the press may have access and proceedings that may be kept confidential.

The prevailing opinion in the *Gannett* case avoided these questions by ruling (1) that any right of access under the first amendment is at best a qualified right; and (2) that in the circumstances of the particular case, the right could be subordinated to the defendant's right to keep the pretrial hearing closed in order that he might later receive a fair public trial, unprejudiced by the disclosure of damaging but inadmissible evidence.[73] This deliberate avoidance of the root question enabled Justice Powell to join in the opinion of the Court while separately asserting a right of access,[74] and Justice Rehnquist to join while separately asserting that the first amendment gives no such right.[75]

The *Gannett* case provoked screams of outrage from the press and much debate among judges, lawyers, and legal scholars.[76] The aftermath brought to light — perhaps the decision even induced — a number of rulings closing the trial of a criminal charge in a state court.[77]

One such ruling came before the Supreme Court of the United States at the last Term as *Richmond Newspapers, Inc. v. Virginia*.[78] The ruling, which was made at the fourth murder trial of a defendant in an antiquated rural courthouse, was related to events at the first three trials, but the record is muddy and the trial court offered no substantial explanation

---

[73] Gannett Co. v. DePasquale, 443 U.S. 368, 392 (1979).

[74] *Id.* at 397–403 (Powell, J., concurring).

[75] *Id.* at 403–06 (Rehnquist, J., concurring).

[76] *See, e.g.*, Richmond Newspapers, Inc. v. Virginia, 100 S. Ct. 2814, 2841 n.1 (1980) (Blackmun, J., concurring in the judgment) (collecting sources); Lewis, *Decision in the Dark*, N.Y. Times, July 5, 1979, at A17, col. 1; N.Y. Times, July 4, 1979, at A8, col. 4; note 97 *infra*.

[77] *See, e.g.*, State v. Leger, No. 79CR6272 (N.C. Super. Ct. Aug. 21, 1979); Rapid City Journal Co. v. Circuit Court, 283 N.W.2d 563 (S.D. 1979) (voir dire proceedings closed). Some trial courts have closed trials to the press but not the public. *See, e.g.*, People v. Sullivan, No. 3721-79 (N.Y. Sup. Ct. Aug. 1, 1979); People v. Worth, No. 79-C13 (W. Va. Cir. Ct. July 24, 1979).

[78] 100 S. Ct. 2814 (1980), *discussed in The Supreme Court, 1979 Term*, 94 HARV. L. REV. 75, 149–59 (1980).

for the ruling. When the local press asked the Supreme Court of Virginia to open the trial to public and press, that court summarily denied relief upon the bare citation of *Gannett Co. v. DePasquale*.[79]

The U.S. Supreme Court reversed, 7–1, holding that "[a]bsent an overriding interest articulated in findings," the first amendment requires that "the trial of a criminal case must be open to the public."[80] There was no opinion of the Court.

The full significance of *Richmond Newspapers* waits for the future. In a concurring opinion Justice Stevens hailed the decision for reading a right of access into the first amendment: "This is a watershed case. Until today the Court has accorded virtually absolute protection to the dissemination of information or ideas, but never before has it squarely held that the acquisition of newsworthy matter is entitled to any constitutional protection whatsoever."[81]

The observation appears to be wishful thinking — or an effort to persuade lower courts to so interpret the decision. The principal opinion, which was delivered by the Chief Justice, begins the analysis with a detailed recital of Anglo-American legal history designed to show that "throughout its evolution, the trial has been open to all who care to observe."[82] From this "unbroken, uncontradicted history, supported by reasons as valid today as in centuries past,"[83] he concluded that "a presumption of openness inheres in the very nature of a criminal trial under our system of justice."[84] Our system of justice is made up of some rights guaranteed in the Federal Constitution, but others are secured under state common law, statutes, and constitutions, and also by federal judge-made law applicable only in the federal courts. In bridging the gap between our system of justice and a first amendment guaran-

---

[79] 100 S. Ct. at 2820 (plurality opinion).
[80] *Id.* at 2830.
[81] *Id.* (Stevens, J., concurring).
[82] 100 S. Ct. at 2821 (plurality opinion).
[83] *Id.* at 2825.
[84] *Id.*

tee, the Chief Justice included two passages that lend color to Justice Stevens' conclusion:

> "[T]he First Amendment goes beyond protection of the press and the self-expression of individuals to prohibit government from limiting the stock of information from which members of the public may draw." *First National Bank of Boston v. Bellotti*, 435 U.S. 765, 783 (1978). . . .
> It is not crucial whether we describe this right to attend criminal trials to hear, see, and communicate observations concerning them as a "right of access," cf. *Gannett, supra,* 443 U.S., at 397 (POWELL, J., concurring); *Saxbe v. Washington Post Co.,* 417 U.S. 843 (1974); *Pell v. Procunier,* 417 U.S. 817 (1974), or a "right to gather information," for we have recognized that "without some protection for seeking out the news, freedom of the press could be eviscerated." *Branzburg v. Hayes,* 408 U.S. 665, 681 (1972).[85]

The first of these passages takes out of context a sentence from an opinion of the Court by Justice Powell explaining a ruling that the first amendment secures the right of a banking corporation voluntarily to spend money for political advertising because the advertising adds to the "stock of information from which members of the public may draw."[86] The sentence had nothing to do with the stock of information to be supplied by government.

The second passage is more puzzling. Does it mean that nothing turns on whether one chooses to describe the right to attend criminal trials as a "right of access" rather than as a "right to gather information"? Or does the passage mean that one may recognize the right to attend criminal trials without describing it as a right of either "access" or "information"? In two cases cited in the second passage, the Court had rejected a newspaper's claim of a right of access to prisoners in a penitentiary on the ground that "the First Amendment does not guarantee the press a constitutional right of special access

---

[85] *Id.* at 2827 (parallel citations and footnotes omitted).
[86] First Nat'l Bank v. Bellotti, 435 U.S. 765, 783 (1978).

to information not available to the public generally."[87] Four Justices, including Justice Stevens, had dissented in *Saxbe*[88] and *Pell*.[89] If the Chief Justice had intended to adopt their view in *Richmond Newspapers*, it would have been appropriate to have cited the dissenting opinions. The general citation to the cases prefaced by "cf." suggests that the Chief Justice intended to imply that *Richmond Newspapers* could be decided without reviving the general "right of access" question.

Moreover, the "unbroken, uncontradicted history" of open criminal trials can logically support the Chief Justice's conclusion even though the first amendment confers no affirmative right of access to information about government in the usual sense of the words. As the law matures, the rudimentary distinctions between action and inaction, right and privilege, or aggressive interference and withholding of benefit become too simple. Closing the door of a courtroom that has always been open can be realistically viewed as interference with observation and public reporting rather than as preservation of the confidentiality of one variety of official business.[90] That this is the gist of the decision is suggested by the Chief Justice's assertion that "[w]hat this means in the context of trials is that the First Amendment guarantees of speech and press, standing alone, prohibit government from summarily closing courtroom doors which had long been open to the public at the time that amendment was adopted."[91]

Later in the opinion the Chief Justice refers to "streets, sidewalks and parks" as "places traditionally open, where First

---

[87] Pell v. Procunier, 417 U.S. 817, 833 (1974) (quoting Branzburg v. Hayes, 408 U.S. 665, 684 (1972)); *see* Saxbe v. Washington Post Co., 417 U.S. 843, 850 (1974).

[88] 417 U.S. 843 (1974).

[89] 417 U.S. 817 (1974).

[90] A parallel line of argument was rejected in Harris v. McRae, 100 S. Ct. 2671 (1980), *discussed in The Supreme Court, 1979 Term*, 94 HARV. L. REV. 75, 96–107 (1980), where the Court held that withholding federal reimbursement for medically necessary abortions, while paying for all other medically necessary operations, should be judged as a simple withholding of benefit.

[91] 100 S. Ct. at 2827 (plurality opinion).

Amendment rights may be exercised," and goes on to assert
that "a trial courtroom also is a public place where the people
generally — and the representatives of the media — have a
right to be present."[92] The analogy is presented in an effort
to draw upon the right of peaceable assembly to support the
ruling. I find it much more persuasive of the proposition that
cutting off opportunities previously and generally provided by
the state may be treated as interference with the activity rather
than as a refusal to facilitate such activity. A municipality
need not create parks or auditoriums for speakers, but if they
exist and have long been so used, the municipality cannot
without specific overriding justification withdraw them from
particular speakers or subjects of discussion.[93]

In sum, although it seems unlikely that the majority is as
ready to retreat from earlier expressions as Justice Stevens
would have us believe, the Court was so badly splintered and
the opinion delivered by the Chief Justice is woven of so many
strands that the decision can stand only for the proposition
that the public has a federal constitutional right to attend the
kind of criminal trial that has historically been open to the
public, unless circumstances justify its closure.

The question whether the first amendment grants press and
public a true right of access to information about federal governmental activities or to information in the possession of the
government will surely recur. The task of developing a body
of law delimiting such a right appears overwhelming. Yet
recognition of the right may well be essential if the first amendment is to continue to serve the basic function of keeping the
people informed about their government. In the beginning
citizens could be reasonably sure of obtaining the facts and of
communicating with each other in the ways necessary for self-
government, provided that government was denied the power
of censorship, that the printing presses were all open to use,
and that individuals could speak, write and publish, and

---

[92] *Id.* at 2828.
[93] *See* pp. 56–59 *infra*. *See also* Cass, *First Amendment Access to Government Facilities*, 65 VA. L. REV. 1287 (1979).

associate with one another without fear of reprisal by rulers or elected representatives. This condition no longer prevails with respect to many activities of the federal government. Because of their scale and complexity, coupled with the interdependence of all aspects of society, government itself is often the chief, if not the only, source of information for the people about the conduct of those who are supposed to be the people's agents. The central problem today is how to deal with governmental secrecy and — all too often — with governmental deception. Justice Brennan's concurring opinion in *Richmond Newspapers*[94] may yet become the law of the first amendment.

The *Richmond Newspapers* case also illustrates several broader and worrisome characteristics of constitutional adjudication under the Burger Court.

First, the first amendment challenge to a closed trial arose only because of the egregious shortcoming of another arm of government. Protection of the public interest in open trials should come from the state appellate courts and from the supervisory power of the U.S. Supreme Court over the inferior federal courts.[95] For the Supreme Court of Virginia to dismiss the newspaper's application upon the bare citation of the *Gannett* case seems grossly inadequate in its neglect of state law. Other state courts have recognized the responsibility.[96] To correct an unwarranted departure from "our system of justice" — and perhaps to escape further pummeling by the press — the Court was drawn into creating yet another new federal constitutional right.

Second, the *Gannett* and *Richmond Newspapers* cases taken together illustrate a characteristic that I regard as a major fault of the present Justices — their insistence upon

---

[94] 100 S. Ct. at 2832–39 (Brennan, J., concurring).

[95] *See The Supreme Court, 1978 Term*, 93 HARV. L. REV. 60, 70–72 (1979).

[96] *See, e.g.*, Phoenix Newspapers, Inc. v. Jennings, 107 Ariz. 557, 490 P.2d 563 (1971); Detroit Free Press v. Recorder's Court Judge, 49 U.S.L.W. 2104 (Mich. July 31, 1980); Rhoades v. State, 102 Neb. 750, 169 N.W. 433 (1918), *cited in* Fenner & Koley, *The Rights of the Press and the Closed Court Criminal Proceeding*, 57 NEB. L. REV. 442, 485 (1978); Federated Publications v. Kurtz, 49 U.S.L.W. 2103 (Wash. July 24, 1980).

individual opinions and consequently their failure to achieve
and articulate the consensuses necessary to maintain an ever-
growing yet continuous body of law. The *Gannett* case evoked
five opinions. The majority and dissenting opinions were necessary, but the others created confusion. The clashing concurring opinions by Justices Powell and Rehnquist staked out
— and apparently sought to induce lower courts to adopt —
propositions that the Court had properly pretermitted. Later,
several Justices ventured inconsistent public discussion of the
holding.[97]

The *Richmond Newspapers* case evoked seven opinions
among eight Justices: six opinions supporting the judgment
and one dissent. The variety must be attributed partly to
unwillingness to yield personal preferences and partly to the
desire to influence the future. Justice Stevens' insistence that
the decision "unequivocally holds that an arbitrary interference
with access to important information is an abridgment of the
freedoms of speech and of the press protected by the First
Amendment"[98] falls in the latter category, as does the eloquent
concurring opinion of Justice Brennan, who was joined by
Justice Marshall. Justice Blackmun reasserted the view that
the sixth amendment gives the public a right to open trial, and

---

[97] First, Chief Justice Burger on August 8, 1979 in an interview with, ironically,
a reporter from the Gannett News Service was quoted as saying, "[T]he opinion
referred to pretrial proceedings only." N.Y. Times, Aug. 9, 1979, at A17, col. 1.
Three weeks later, Justice Blackmun, who dissented in *Gannett*, told a group of
federal judges that "despite what my colleague, the Chief Justice, has said," the
opinion authorized the closing of all trials. N.Y. Times, Sept. 4, 1979, at A15, col.
1. On September 8, 1979, Justice Stevens said that "the normal reason for an *in
camera* proceeding is to prevent the jury from having access to inadmissible matter;
that reason could not possibly motivate an order excluding the public from the
proceedings that take place in the presence of the jury," thereby implying that he too
would limit *Gannett* to pretrial proceedings. N.Y. Times, Sept. 9, 1979, at A41, col.
1. On August 13, 1979, Justice Powell suggested that judges might be "a bit pre-
mature" in interpreting *Gannett* to allow exclusion of the press from full trials while
allowing other members of the public to remain. N.Y. Times, Aug. 14, 1979, at A13,
col. 1; N.Y. Times, Sept. 4, 1979, at A15, col. 1. *See also* Brennan, *Address*, 32
RUTGERS L. REV. 173, 181–82 (1979).

[98] 100 S. Ct. at 2831 (Stevens, J., concurring).

then concluded as a grudging and unreasoned "secondary position" that "the First Amendment must provide some measure of protection for public access to the trial."[99] For all seven Justices to have joined in a single opinion deciding no more than reversal required and leaving other questions to the future would have made a more constructive contribution to the relevant body of law.

Implicit in this criticism is the judgment that nurturing a coherent body of constitutional law is usually more important for members of the highest court than asserting individual views or staking out claims on the future. In an era of social flux there is need for creativity and change in the body of law. A coherent body of law need not be static. Only a logical absolutist supposes that judges must choose between total disregard of and rigid adherence to precedent. In the final analysis, moreover, it is the recognition of responsibility to a body of law that legitimates constitutional adjudication as the work of a court rather than the elitist edicts of Platonic Guardians.

Third, nurturing a body of law requires more attention than Chief Justice Burger's opinion in *Richmond Newspapers* gives to fitting new decisions into the body of precedent. The opinion makes no effort to square the ruling with the rationale of *Pell v. Procunier*[100] and *Saxbe v. Washington Post Co.*[101] Nor does it refer to the Chief Justice's own opinion just two years before in *Houchins v. KQED, Inc.*[102] Surely, some

---

[99] *Id.* at 2842 (Blackmun, J., concurring in the judgment).

[100] 417 U.S. 817 (1974).

[101] 417 U.S. 843 (1974).

[102] In *Houchins* v. KQED, Inc., 438 U.S. 1 (1978), the Chief Justice had declared with the support of three colleagues, "Neither the First Amendment nor the Fourteenth Amendment mandates a right of access to government information or sources of information within the government's control." *Id.* at 15 (plurality opinion); *see id.* at 16 (Stewart, J., concurring in the judgment). Justice Blackmun seems to share this view. Justice Blackmun had joined the prevailing opinions in *Pell* and *Saxbe*. He took no part in *Houchins*, but he had noted in *Gannett* that he was not persuaded by the newspaper's arguments under the first amendment. In *Richmond Newspapers*, Justice Blackmun accepted the claim that the first amendment secured "some measure of public access to the trial" only as a secondary position. 100 S. Ct. at 2842 (Blackmun, J., concurring in the judgment).

effort to explain the relation between the decision in *Richmond Newspapers* and those earlier cases was required. While the issue lies further afield and many distinctions are available, one also might have supposed it important for the Court to explain in either *United States v. Snepp* or *Richmond Newspapers* how the ruling that Snepp acted wrongfully in publishing unclassified information about governmental activities is to be reconciled with the new first amendment right of public access to a criminal trial.[103]

B. Speech in Pursuit of Economic Self-Interest

1. The Extension of the First Amendment. — The most venturesome rulings of the Burger Court dealing with freedom of expression have overturned settled law and extended the first amendment to commercial advertising. The key decision is *Virginia State Board of Pharmacy v. Virginia Citizens Consumer Council, Inc.,*[104] where the majority held unconstitutional a statute prohibiting pharmacists from advertising the prices at which they would sell prescription drugs.

The opinion underscores the problems of the Burger Court in developing a coherent approach to the first amendment. The Court paid little attention to building a systematic body of law, but instead engaged in particularistic and pragmatic balancing. The applicable precedents went far to establish that commercial advertising is not protected by the first amendment.[105] In any reconsideration of those rulings, the first question to ask would seem to be whether commercial advertising is enough like other "speech" protected by the first amendment to be given the same protection. If so, the case would be governed by the well-established principle that direct suppression is permissible, if ever, only because of overwhelming public necessity. If not, the advertising would be governed by the principle that a regulatory law is constitutional if it can

---

[103] The *Snepp* case is discussed at pp. 9–13 *supra*.

[104] 425 U.S. 748 (1976).

[105] *E.g.*, Valentine v. Chrestensen, 316 U.S. 52 (1942); Breard v. Alexandria, 341 U.S. 622 (1951).

reasonably be supposed to contribute to the effectuation of some rational view of the public interest. In the latter event, statutes prohibiting advertising of the price of prescription drugs would surely be upheld. Indeed, such laws had been sustained for decades against attacks under the due process and equal protection clauses.[106]

In the *Pharmacists* case, the Court was unwilling to uphold the foolish statute despite the supporting precedents, but it was also unable in good conscience to apply to commercial advertising the principles applicable to other kinds of speech. The philosophical and political foundations of first amendment doctrine scarcely extend to an offer to enter into a private commercial transaction. Given the dilemma, the Court broke the category of protected expressions down into subcategories. The advertiser's interest in publicizing his wares and prices, Justice Blackmun said, is primarily economic; but this does not render his interest insignificant for the purposes of the first amendment. The consumer's interest in the free flow of commercial information "may be as keen, if not keener by far, than his interest in the day's most urgent political debate. . . . It could mean the alleviation of physical pain or the enjoyment of basic necessities."[107] Accordingly, it was held that the first amendment does not deny "all protection" to "speech which does 'no more than propose a commercial transaction.'"[108] But, the Court cautioned, "[W]e have not held that it is wholly undifferentiable from other forms. There are commonsense differences . . . ."[109]

The interests affected by the statute were overwhelmingly economic. The gist of Justice Blackmun's criticism was that

---

[106] *See, e.g.*, Williamson v. Lee Optical Co., 348 U.S. 483 (1955); Semler v. Oregon State Bd. of Dental Examiners, 294 U.S. 608 (1935); *cf.* Head v. New Mexico Bd. of Examiners in Optometry, 374 U.S. 424 (1963) (state statute regulating advertising of optometrists' services held not to violate 14th amendment and commerce clause).

[107] 425 U.S. at 763–64.

[108] *Id.* at 762 (quoting Pittsburgh Press Co. v. Pittsburgh Comm'n on Human Relations, 413 U.S. 376, 385 (1973)).

[109] 425 U.S. at 771 n.24.

such statutes would interfere with the free operation of the market. The adverse effect upon consumers was less than the impact of legislation authorizing resale price maintenance. It is hardly surprising, therefore, that commentators have taxed the Court with reviving the philosophy of *Lochner v. New York*[110] in the guise of first amendment doctrine.[111]

The bench and bar did not have to wait long to witness the consequences of breaking down the category "speech" in order to protect particular communications to which the Court was unwilling to extend full protection under the principles theretofore controlling adjudication under the first amendment. *Young v. American Mini Theatres, Inc.*[112] grew out of a challenge to an "anti-skid row" ordinance adopted by Detroit in 1962, which forbade using property for certain businesses if located within 1,000 feet of two other establishments in the same category; included in this list of businesses were dance halls, pool rooms, public lodging houses, shoe shine parlors, bars, and pawn shops. The theory was that the concentration of such uses tends to attract undesirable transients, to increase prostitution and other crimes, and to depress the value of property and quality of life in the entire neighborhood. In 1972, the ordinance was amended to add adult theaters and adult book stores to the list of establishments that should not be operated in the proximity of each other.

The Detroit ordinance may well make good sense. Putting the first amendment to one side, it is a promising remedy for what many see as grave social and economic blight. The difficulty is that one cannot put the amendment aside without permitting some regulation of speech because of its content and the consequences of the ideas and images expressed. The established principle had been that a court should not attempt to differentiate or allow the state to differentiate the value of particular messages protected by the first amendment. In

---

[110] 198 U.S. 45 (1905).

[111] *E.g.*, Jackson & Jeffries, *Commercial Speech: Economic Due Process and the First Amendment*, 65 VA. L. REV. 1 (1979).

[112] 427 U.S. 50 (1976).

American Mini Theatres, however, Justice Stevens, speaking for the plurality, made it plain that even though the pictures to be exhibited were within the scope of first amendment protection, the plurality judged them to belong, like commercial advertising, in the category of second-class speech.

> [F]ew of us would march our sons and daughters off to war to preserve the citizen's right to see "Specified Sexual Activities" exhibited in the theaters of our choice. Even though the First Amendment protects communication in this area from total suppression, we hold that the State may legitimately use the content of these materials as the basis for placing them in a different classification from other motion pictures.[113]

Few of us would march our sons or daughters off to war to preserve the citizen's right to see pictures of American Nazis marching in uniform in Skokie, Illinois, or to hear advocacy of Stalinist Communism, or to read advertisements stating the price of prescription drugs. That test is both unreasoning and insufficient. Justice Stevens also suggests that a line may be drawn between the political and the sexually explicit.[114] Only three other Justices have approved this classification.[115] Still, one is bound to wonder where the process of particularization commenced in the *Pharmacists* case will stop.

From the proposition that sexually explicit adult movies are only second-class speech, the plurality proceeded directly to the conclusion that the zoning restriction was sufficiently justified by the city's interest in preserving the character of its neighborhoods.

> The record discloses a factual basis for the Common Council's conclusion that this kind of restriction will have the desired effect [of preventing the deterioration of neighborhoods]. It is not our function to appraise the wisdom of its decision to require adult theatres to be separated rather than concentrated in the same areas. . . . Moreover, the city must be allowed

---

[113] *Id.* at 70–71 (plurality opinion).

[114] *Id.*

[115] *Id.* at 52; *id.* at 73 n.1 (Powell, J., concurring).

a reasonable opportunity to experiment with solutions to admittedly serious problems.[116]

Experiment with regulating speech! Surely, the words are those of advocates of judicial self-restraint. They would flow logically from some of Justice Frankfurter's opinions[117] (although intuition tells me that he would never have written the words). The teaching seems to be that in dealing with second-class speech, or, at least, one form of second-class speech, the Court will not make its own findings concerning the relevant social and economic conditions or substitute its own judgment as to the consequences of the challenged law for the judgment of the legislative body.[118]

Contrast the approach taken in the *Pharmacists* case, where at the very same Term as *American Mini Theatres*, the Court followed an altogether different course. Virginia sought to justify its statute upon the ground that price advertising threatens the public interest in maintaining a "high degree of professionalism on the part of licensed pharmacists."[119] Justice Blackmun concluded "on close inspection"[120] that the justification was insufficient, partly because professionalism could be enforced by direct regulation, partly because the advertising ban did not prevent the pharmacists from cutting corners, and partly because it is impermissibly paternalistic to protect consumers against the danger of patronizing price-conscious rather than service-conscious pharmacists by denying them information about where they can get a lower price. On balance, the Justice concluded, the state may not seek to establish and

---

[116] 427 U.S. at 71 (plurality opinion) (footnote omitted).

[117] *E.g.*, West Virginia State Bd. of Educ. v. Barnette, 319 U.S. 624, 646 (1943) (Frankfurter, J., dissenting) (due process clause should not allow the Court to strike down state law designed to reach the "legitimate legislative end" of "promotion of good citizenship" by requiring students to salute the flag and to say the Pledge of Allegiance).

[118] The above approach is consistently followed in dealing with laws that regulate business activity. For a collection of relevant cases, see Cox, *The Role of Congress in Constitutional Determinations*, 40 U. CIN. L. REV. 199, 206–11, 217–24 (1971).

[119] 425 U.S. at 766.

[120] *Id.* at 769.

safeguard professional standards by "keeping the public in ignorance of the entirely lawful terms that competing pharmacists are offering."[121]

Why is it a function of the Court to appraise for itself the effects and thus the wisdom of prohibiting price advertisements by pharmacists while it defers as in economic regulation cases to state experimentation with the effects of a zoning ordinance requiring the dispersal of establishments offering "adult" books and theaters? There may be an explanation, but none was offered in the opinions. Nor did the Court explain in the *Pharmacists* case why it felt free to evaluate and balance overwhelmingly economic interests that it would have left to the legislature under a statute calling for retail price maintenance.

I stress the point because the delineation of the respective institutional functions of the judicial and legislative branches is essential to the development of a coherent body of principles governing constitutional adjudication. Whenever a constitutional right is less than absolute, the constitutionality of a law restricting its exercise may depend upon an appraisal of (1) existing social, economic, or political conditions and (2) the tendency of the law actually to promote the public interest claimed to justify the restriction. During the era of judicial self-restraint such judgments were left to Congress and the state legislatures under the presumption of constitutionality and the accompanying rule that legislative findings of fact must be accepted unless proved to be irrational.[122] The evolution of "strict review" under the preferred rights approach to the first amendment, and later under the equal protection clause, appears to contemplate more searching judicial inquiry, but the Warren Court made no serious effort to address the question.[123]

Inconsistency marks the pronouncements of the Burger Court. The contrast between *Virginia State Board of Phar-*

---

[121] *Id.* at 770.

[122] *E.g.*, McGowan v. Maryland, 366 U.S. 420, 426 (1961); United States v. Carolene Prods. Co., 304 U.S. 144, 152–53 (1938).

[123] *See* Cox, *supra* note 118, at 211–24.

macy and *American Mini Theatres* is one example. In *Land-mark Communications, Inc. v. Virginia*, the Chief Justice de-clared that "[d]eference to a legislative finding cannot limit judicial inquiry when First Amendment rights are at stake."[124] On the other hand, in another case, which held that the first amendment permits a broadcast licensee to adopt a blanket rule refusing to sell time for spot pronouncements upon public issues, the Chief Justice relied heavily on the judgments of Congress.[125]

The development of principles for the consistent resolution of these recurring questions of institutional relationship would ease the problems of counsel and lower courts and contribute immeasurably to the coherence of a body of constitutional law.[126]

---

[124] 435 U.S. 829, 843 (1978).

[125] Columbia Broadcasting Sys., Inc. v. Democratic Nat'l Comm., 412 U.S. 94 (1973). Similarly, even though a racial classification is subject to strict scrutiny, the Chief Justice deferred to the findings of Congress in upholding legislation requiring each grant of funds to local government for public works to set aside 10% for "minority-business enterprises." Fullilove v. Klutznik, 100 S. Ct. 2758 (1980), *discussed in The Supreme Court, 1979 Term*, 94 HARV. L. REV. 75, 125–38 (1980). In other strict scrutiny cases under the equal protection clause, however, the Court has required proof of the facts alleged to support the legislation or has examined the evidence for itself. *E.g.*, Craig v. Boren, 429 U.S. 190 (1976); Regents of the Univ. of Cal. v. Bakke, 438 U.S. 265, 310–11 (opinion of Powell, J.).

[126] Determining the relationship between court and legislature with respect to the relevant conditions and the tendencies of a legislative remedy for a social evil requires examining a number of specific questions, on some of which Justices from time to time express opinions, but which the Court has never systematically confronted and attempted to resolve:

(1) When, if ever, are express legislative findings required to supply the justifi-cation for a law subject to more than minimal judicial scrutiny?

(2) To what extent will the Court accept express and/or implied legislative find-ings? Is the standard the same in all cases of more than minimal scrutiny?

(3) When, if ever, do counsel supporting the constitutionality of a measure subject to more than minimal judicial scrutiny have a duty to "prove" the facts showing justification?

(4) Is the necessary "proof" to be established by evidence in the trial court or by argument in a "Brandeis brief"?

(5) If the proof is provided by evidence, what weight will be given the trial court's findings of fact?

2. Policing for Deception and Overreaching. — In extending the first amendment to commercial advertising the Court was bound to recognize that protection of consumers against deception, overreaching, and other unfair trade practices would require a degree of governmental scrutiny of advertisements and sales talks utterly intolerable in the political arena or in the arts and sciences. This was reason enough to acknowledge that commercial advertising must be differentiated in constitutional terms from other speech. All the Justices of the present Court have therefore agreed, with minor differences of phrasing and emphasis, that inaccurate commercial messages are not protected by the first amendment.[127] Seemingly, even prior submission for some kinds of government scrutiny may be required.[128]

Difficulties and differences of opinion arise in applying a special set of rules to "commercial speech" as expression separable from fully protected speech, on the one side, and economic activity, on the other. *Ohralik v. Ohio State Bar Association*[129] sustained disciplinary action against an attorney who engaged in personal solicitation of potential tort plaintiffs because of the risks of fraud, undue influence, overreaching, or other forms of vexatious conduct. *In re Primus*,[130] however, concluded after more exacting scrutiny that personal solicitation of a client on behalf of an association seeking to promote political and ideological goals is entitled to full first amendment protection, at least when legal assistance is available to the client without charge and the attorney will receive no direct monetary benefit from the particular case. The difference is real enough in these two instances, but there may

---

[127] Friedman v. Rogers, 440 U.S. 1 (1979); Bates v. State Bar, 483 U.S. 350, 383 (1977); Virginia State Bd. of Pharmacy v. Virginia Citizens Consumer Council, Inc., 425 U.S. 748, 770–72 & n.24, 775–81 (1976).

[128] Central Hudson Gas & Elec. Corp. v. Public Serv. Comm'n, 100 S. Ct. 2343, 2354 n.13 (1980); Virginia State Bd. of Pharmacy v. Virginia Citizens Consumer Council, Inc., 425 U.S. 748, 771 n.24 (1976). *See also* Bates v. State Bar, 433 U.S. 350, 383 (1977).

[129] 436 U.S. 447 (1978).

[130] 436 U.S. 412 (1978).

be ground for Justice Rehnquist's doubt about the Court's
ability to maintain a principled distinction between "civil liberties lawyers" and "ambulance chasers."[131]

  Friedman v. Rogers,[132] if the opinion is to be read literally,
suggests that very little protection will be accorded commercial
speech when the justification for restraint is a risk of deception.
The challenge was to a Texas statute prohibiting the practice
of optometry under a trade name. The Court upheld the
statute because the consumer's association of a trade name
with price and quality creates "a significant possibility" of
misleading the public given the ease with which trade names
may change.[133] Justice Blackmun, dissenting, protested that
the Court was retreating from *Virginia Pharmacists*.[134] The
criticism is not without foundation. One would suppose that
competition among pharmacists based upon vigorous advertising of price creates "a significant possibility" of injuring consumers through deterioration of professional service.

  The key to the decision, however, may well be the futility
of attempting to maintain a general constitutional distinction
between commercial advertising and other commercial activity. The thrust of the Texas statute is to protect the "professional" optometrists who practice as individuals or partner-
ships at a limited number of locations against the "commercial"
optometrists who work in chains of establishments under a
common name and management, and with greater efficiency.
Texas, without violating the fourteenth amendment, might
have prohibited the operation of an optometrical establishment
by anyone other than licensed optometrists.[135] It would seem
foolish to distinguish the two statutes because the statute in
Friedman v. Rogers can be labeled a restriction upon "speech."
For this reason, and also because only slight protection was
accorded to speech in *Friedman v. Rogers*, some scholars have

---

[131] *Id.* at 440 (Rehnquist, J., dissenting).

[132] 440 U.S. 1 (1979).

[133] *Id.* at 13.

[134] *Id.* at 19–28 (Blackmun, J., concurring in part and dissenting in part).

[135] North Dakota State Bd. of Pharmacy v. Snyder's Drug Stores, Inc., 414 U.S.
156 (1973).

inferred that the Court will continue to retreat from the doctrine of the *Virginia Pharmacists* case.[136]

3. *Policing Because of the Response to a Truthful Message.*
— The extension of the first amendment to commercial speech raised new problems under the settled doctrine that the amendment, subject to few exceptions, bars restricting speech or related forms of communication because of the dangerous tendency of the ideas expressed. The restriction of advertising and the prohibition of certain forms are effective methods of promoting the public interest by reducing the consumption of harmful products or products in short supply. The federal law prohibiting the use of radio or television to promote the sale of cigarettes[137] and the statutes adopted by some states to bar advertising alcoholic beverages are the most familiar instances.[138] *Virginia Pharmacists* put such laws in question, for they would be unconstitutional if the established first amendment doctrine applies to commercial advertising.

The Court's initial response appeared to apply the usual rule. In *Linmark Associates, Inc. v. Township of Willingboro*,[139] the town of Willingboro, N.J., had forbidden real estate agents to post "For Sale" and "Sold" signs upon residential premises for the purpose of stemming what the Township Council perceived as panic selling and white flight from a previously racially integrated community. The unanimous opinion[140] observed that the town had misconceived the situation and that the ordinance was not shown to be necessary, but it held the ordinance unconstitutional because of a "far more basic defect": "The Council has sought to restrict the

---

[136] *See, e.g.*, Jackson & Jeffries, *supra* note 111; G. GUNTHER, CONSTITUTIONAL LAW 1395–97 (10th ed. 1980).

[137] Federal Cigarette Labelling and Advertising Act, 15 U.S.C. §§ 1331–1340 (1965), *as amended by* Public Health Cigarette Smoking Act of 1969, Pub. L. No. 91-222, § 2, 84 Stat. 87 (1970).

[138] *See, e.g.*, FLA. STAT. ANN. § 561.42(10)–(12) (West Supp. 1980); MASS. GEN. LAWS ANN. ch. 138, § 24 (West 1974); UTAH CODE ANN. §§ 32-7-26 to -28 (1965 & Supp. 1979).

[139] 431 U.S. 85 (1977).

[140] *Id.* at 96.

free flow of these data because it fears that otherwise homeowners will make decisions inimical to what the Council views
as the homeowners' self-interest and the corporate interest of
the township: they will choose to leave town."[141] A few sen-
tences later, Justice Marshall declared, "It is precisely this kind
of choice between the dangers of suppressing information, and
the dangers of its misuse if it is freely available, that the First
Amendment makes for us."[142] There followed a quotation
from Justice Brandeis' famous opinion in *Whitney v. California*[143] refining the clear and present danger test.

Last Term, the Court took a new tack less solicitous of
commercial speech in *Central Hudson Gas & Electric Corp.
v. Public Service Commission*,[144] even though it struck down
the particular restriction. The New York Public Service Commission had prohibited all electrical utilities from advertising
to promote the purchase of utility services, intending thereby
to limit the demand for energy. In reviewing the order under
the first amendment the majority laid down three requirements
that a state must satisfy in order to justify a measure restricting
nondeceptive commercial advertising. First, the restriction
must serve a substantial state interest. Second, the measure
must directly advance the substantial state interest. Third,
the restriction must be no broader than is necessary to advance
the state's interest.[145] In *Central Hudson* the Court concluded
that the saving of energy was a substantial state interest and
that the prohibition of promotional advertising served that
interest,[146] but it held that the order must be set aside because
a narrower order might have been written, one that had not

---

[141] *Id.*

[142] *Id.* at 97 (quoting Virginia State Bd. of Pharmacy v. Virginia Citizens Consumer Council, Inc., 425 U.S. 748, 770 (1976)).

[143] 274 U.S. 357, 377 (1927) (Brandeis, J., concurring).

[144] 100 S. Ct. 2343 (1980), *discussed in The Supreme Court, 1979 Term*, 94 HARV.
L. REV. 75, 159–68 (1980).

[145] 100 S. Ct. at 2351.

[146] *Id.* at 2352–53.

been proved inadequate to further the interest in energy conservation.[147]

The most striking aspects of the case are the weight of the burden put upon the state and the degree to which judicial opinion is substituted for the state regulatory authority. The order was overbroad, the Court ruled, because it forbade the promotion of electric devices that might be used in replacement of devices using other forms of energy. "In the absence of authoritative findings to the contrary, we must credit as *within the realm of possibility* the claim that electric heat can be an efficient alternative in some circumstances."[148] The order might be too severe; perhaps it would suffice to require statements about cost and relative efficiency. Or the Public Service Commission might preview all advertisements before publication in order to ensure that they would not defeat energy conservation.[149] Such close judicial analysis of policy alternatives in utility regulation, with the burden put upon the state to foresee and negate all the alternatives that the Court can imagine, seems a far cry from the plurality's declaration that the state "must be allowed a reasonable opportunity to experiment with solutions to admittedly serious problems" in regulating the sale of books and exhibitions of motion pictures dealing with sex.[150]

Viewed more broadly, however, *Central Hudson* appears to indicate that a restriction upon commercial advertising will be valid despite the first amendment when the regulation can be shown to be necessary to promote a substantial state interest.[151]

Although "commercial advertising" was formerly denied

---

[147] *Id.* at 2353–54.

[148] *Id.* at 2353 (emphasis added).

[149] *Id.* at 2354 & n.13.

[150] Young v. American Mini Theatres, Inc., 427 U.S. 50, 71 (1976).

[151] *See, e.g.,* Capital Broadcasting Co. v. Acting Attorney Gen., 405 U.S. 1000 (1972) (upholding a prohibition upon the broadcast of cigarette advertisements but decided before the *Virginia Pharmacists* case), *summarily aff'g* 333 F. Supp. 582 (D.D.C. 1971).

first amendment protection, other communications primarily designed to induce private decisions in the private economic sector that would promote the speaker's economic interest had long been granted that protection.[152] Of these activities, peaceful labor picketing is the most important, and also the most difficult to fit into a coherent body of first amendment law.

NLRB v. Retail Store Employees Local 1001[153] furnishes an unusually interesting example of the difficulty because it was decided on the same day as *Central Hudson*, and in both cases Justice Powell delivered the opinion of the Court. During a labor dispute with Safeco, an underwriter of real estate title insurance, Local 1001 picketed the premises of five local companies that searched titles, performed escrow services and sold Safeco, and only Safeco, insurance policies. The pickets appealed to the customers of the local company to support them by canceling their insurance policies. The Court sustained the NLRB holding that the secondary consumer picketing constituted an unfair labor practice because it coerced the secondary employer.[154] A five-man majority also rejected the union's plea that its general appeal to the public through picketing was protected by the first amendment.

Once again the Justices disagreed in their reasons. The five votes required three opinions. None is wholly satisfactory.

Justice Powell, speaking for himself, the Chief Justice, and Justices Stewart and Rehnquist, upheld the ban because the activity was in furtherance of "unlawful objectives," *i.e.*, inducing customers not to patronize a secondary employer in order to induce it to join in putting economic pressure on the primary employer with whom the union had its dispute. The

---

[152] *E.g.*, Thomas v. Collins, 323 U.S. 516 (1945); NLRB v. Virginia Elec. & Power Co., 314 U.S. 469 (1941); Thornhill v. Alabama, 310 U.S. 88 (1940).

[153] 100 S. Ct. 2372 (1980).

[154] *See* 29 U.S.C. § 158(b)(4)(ii)(B) (1976). The decision severely limited NLRB v. Fruit & Vegetable Packers & Warehousemen Local 760 ("Tree Fruits"), 377 U.S. 58 (1964), which held it is not an unfair labor practice for a union involved in a labor dispute with a primary employer to peacefully picket a secondary site so as to persuade consumers to boycott the primary employer's product.

objectives were "unlawful" only in a Pickwickian sense.[155]
The customers violate no law by ceasing to do business with
the secondary employer. The secondary employer violates no
law by ceasing to do business with the primary employer. The
primary employer violates no law by settling the dispute upon
the union's terms. Congress deemed these consequences undesirable because they extend economic warfare by involving
neutrals, but it did not proscribe anything but the appeal to
the customers. This aspect of the case exactly parallels *Central
Hudson*. In both instances the government proscribed a form
of expression appealing to readers or observers because it believed that the message would have an undesirable effect. Yet
in *Central Hudson* the ban was struck down. Justice Powell
offered no reconciliation, perhaps because he regarded the
difference as too obvious for mention.

Justice Stevens recognized that a restriction upon picketing
because of the content and consequences of the message violates the rigid rule forbidding government regulation based
upon the ideas expressed, but he found justification in the
special nature of picketing: "[P]icketing is a mixture of conduct
and communication. In the labor context, it is the conduct
element rather than the particular idea being expressed that
often provides the most persuásive deterrent to third persons
about to enter a business establishment."[156]

I wish that Justice Stevens had elaborated upon "conduct"
and "deterrent." When I pressed a similar argument upon the
Court in the precursor to *Local 1001*,[157] counsel for the
Teamsters Union exhibited photographs of the pickets; they
were slightly built, white-haired and gentle, elderly ladies.
"How," he cried, "did their conduct influence anyone apart
from the ideas expressed?"

---

[155] C. DICKENS, PICKWICK PAPERS ch. 1 (1836–1837); *cf.* L. CARROLL, THROUGH
THE LOOKING GLASS ch. 6 (1872) ("'When I use a word,' Humpty Dumpty said, in
a rather scornful tone, 'it means just what I choose it to mean — neither more nor
less.'").

[156] 100 S. Ct. at 2379 (Stevens, J., concurring).

[157] NLRB v. Fruit & Vegetable Packers & Warehousemen Local 760 ("Tree
Fruits"), 377 U.S. 58 (1964).

To speak of "picketing" simpliciter breeds confusion. Some picketing operates as a signal; it is brigaded with conduct, as Justice Black explained in *Giboney v. Empire Storage & Ice Co.*:[158]

> [A]ll of appellants' activities — their powerful transportation combination, their patrolling, their formation of a picket line warning union men not to cross at peril of their union membership, their publicizing — constituted a single and integrated course of conduct, which was in violation of Missouri's valid law. . . . [Therefore] it is clear that appellants were doing more than exercising a right of free speech or press. *Bakery Drivers Local* v. *Wohl*, 315 U.S. 769, 776–777. They were exercising their economic power together with that of their allies to compel Empire to abide by union rather than by state regulation of trade.[159]

The picket's reliance in such a case is on the sanctions inherent in the discipline and organized economic power of his union.

Quite different is the peaceful picketing that is directed primarily to the general public. Familiar illustrations may be found outside motion picture theaters, restaurants, and beauty parlors where none of the employees are on strike. Theoretically, such picket lines are entitled to the same respect from union members as any other picket line, but as a practical matter the union's sanctions play little part. Prospective patrons who are not union members are left to determine their own course of conduct influenced but not coerced by the knowledge that a labor dispute is in progress. Even union members feel freer to exercise the freedom of choice open to the general public. In such cases, therefore, the success or failure of picketing depends primarily upon the persuasiveness of the pickets' message.

In practice, picketing often is neither as clearly "signal picketing" nor as plainly "publicity picketing" as in these examples, but the categories are sufficiently distinguishable to

---

[158] 336 U.S. 490 (1949).
[159] *Id.* at 498–503.

make the classification useful.[160] In *Local 1001*, the picketing was neither threatening nor a signal setting in motion a prearranged combination to exercise concerted economic power, backed by fear of union discipline; the case seems quite plainly to be one of publicity picketing.

Although Justice Stevens observed that the proscription affects "only that aspect of the union's efforts to communicate its views that calls for an automatic response to a signal, rather than a reasoned response to an idea,"[161] the distinction seems unreal. The signal communicates an idea — here a request to withdraw patronage. Almost any set of symbols or ideas may set in motion a variety of reasoned and unreasoned, deliberate and automatic responses. Does the sickly youth choose Marlboro cigarettes in "reasoned response" to the virility exhibited in the advertising of Marlboro Country? What about the purchaser who selects Noxema shaving cream in response to the blond siren's seductive plea "Take it off. Take it all off."? An automatic or a reasoned response? Surely many, if not most, political speeches include appeals to automatic associations and loyalties as well as to reason. Whether a response is automatic rather than reasoned depends partly upon the temperament of the observer and partly upon his habits, associations, and settled convictions. The character of the response will not serve to measure the availability of protection under the first amendment.

The decision in *Local 1001* can be fitted into the body of first amendment law if picketing is classified with commercial advertising as economic speech. The four-part test promulgated in *Central Hudson* permits a content-based restriction upon commercial advertising when it "directly advances" a "substantial governmental interest" and "is not more extensive than necessary to serve that interest."[162] In terms of the

---

[160] The distinction is elaborated and the formative cases are discussed in Cox, *Strikes, Picketing and the Constitution*, 4 VAND. L. REV. 574 (1951).

[161] 100 S. Ct. at 2379 (Stevens, J., concurring).

[162] See p. 42 *supra*.

political and philosophical foundations of the first amendment, to classify picketing with commercial advertising has considerable merit. Requests for immediate assistance in putting economic pressure upon one with whom the speaker is engaged in driving a private business bargain are readily distinguishable from words looking forward to political action. In the former instance the gain sought and the action requested are both economic. Both occur in the private sector. Advertising urging the purchase of a particular product has much the same character, although there is no element of economic coercion. In choosing a cryptic disposition of the constitutional issue in *Local 1001*, the Court passed over an opportunity to give structure to these aspects of first amendment law.

II. REGULATION OF TIME, PLACE, OR MANNER OF EXPRESSION

Although the first amendment gives speech and related forms of expression virtually absolute protection against restriction based upon the dangerous character of the words, it is often said to allow greater latitude to the state to regulate the time, place, and manner of expression.[163] In truth, the Burger Court has developed and maintained with rare exceptions a principled distinction protective of expression. Restrictions designed to protect opposing public or private interests prejudiced by a particular form of expression, or by expression at a particular time or place, regardless of content, are generally valid if they protect important interests that cannot be secured by less restrictive means. Restrictions upon the time, place, or manner of expression keyed to the subject matter or content have usually been judged and found unconstitutional under the standards applied to laws forbidding or imposing liability for the publication of a class of ideas or information.

---

[163] *E.g.*, Erznoznik v. City of Jacksonville, 422 U.S. 205, 209 (1975); Cox v. Louisiana, 379 U.S. 536, 554 (1965); Kovacs v. Cooper, 336 U.S. 77 (1949).

A. Regulation Because of Consequences Unrelated to Content

Decisions under the first amendment build upon an inherited tradition, but the vision from which many of them spring encompasses greater turbulence and faster changes in society than the intellectual liberalism of the eighteenth and nineteenth centuries. Social, political, or religious activists seeking changes that frighten or annoy all "right-minded" people have little access to the conventional channels of effective expression. For them the best vehicles of expression are sit-ins, picketing, marches, and mass demonstrations. Their language, like their tactics, is often aimed to shock the community. The decisions of the 1960's and 1970's take pains to protect such use of the streets, coarse expletives, affronts to personal and public sensitivities, and other unorthodox methods of expression.

Even without empirical studies it is safe to surmise that the chief danger to freedom of expression by the poor, the unorthodox, and the unpopular lies in licensing ordinances and other general laws that vest wide discretion in local authorities to maintain the peace and public order. Stirred by the civil rights movement and perhaps by the peace movement during the fighting in Vietnam, a majority of the Court has been remarkably alert in developing doctrine that reduces the risks of such abuse. One doctrine, traceable to the 1930's, is that a law requiring a license for the use of the streets or parks for demonstrations, parades, or other forms of expression must explicitly confine the licensing authorities to considerations of traffic control, crowd control, and other such public safety considerations.[164] Broader discretion, it is said, not only creates excessive risk of discrimination but may induce an applicant to mince words that are constitutionally protected, in order to get or keep a license. From there it is only a short step to holding that a man may not be punished for words or for a street demonstration under a broad, general rubric, such as breach of the peace, that leaves wide discretion to the

---

[164] Lovell v. City of Griffin, 303 U.S. 444 (1938).

police, public prosecutors, and judges, and thus invites discrimination based upon distaste for the view expressed rather
than a fair judgment upon the risk of violence.[165] The related
first amendment overbreadth doctrine holds that a speaker or
demonstrator may not be convicted even though his conduct
could be punished constitutionally under a more narrowly
drawn statute if the statute under which he is prosecuted is
drafted in general terms so broad that the authorities could
apply it unconstitutionally to someone else.[166] The decisions
of the 1970's apply these doctrines without significant modification,[167] save for lessening enthusiasm for the doctrine of
overbreadth.[168]

More striking change is evident in the new protection extended to vulgar personal epithets and other offensive words.
The turning point came in *Cohen v. California*,[169] during the
transition from the Warren to the Burger Court. Cohen, a
young man opposed to both conscription for military service
and the war in Vietnam, expressed his protest by walking
about in public places wearing a shirt with the boldly printed
slogan, "FUCK THE DRAFT." He was arrested and convicted for "maliciously and willfully disturb[ing] the peace
. . . by . . . offensive conduct."[170] The Supreme Court reversed
the conviction in an opinion written by the late Justice Harlan,
the most gentle and gentlemanly of Justices and a man of
impeccable taste and sensitivity. Justice Harlan gave three
reasons for concluding that the "First and Fourteenth Amendments must be taken to disable the States from punishing
public utterance of this unseemly expletive in order to maintain

---

165 Cantwell v. Connecticut, 310 U.S. 296 (1940).

166 Gooding v. Wilson, 405 U.S. 518, 520–21 (1972); Thornhill v. Alabama, 310
U.S. 88, 98 (1940). *See generally* Note, *The First Amendment Overbreadth Doctrine*,
83 HARV. L. REV. 844 (1970).

167 *E.g.*, Village of Schaumburg v. Citizens for a Better Environment, 444 U.S.
620 (1980); Hynes v. Mayor & Council, 425 U.S. 610 (1976); Gooding v. Wilson, 405
U.S. 518 (1972).

168 *E.g.*, Broadrick v. Oklahoma, 413 U.S. 601 (1973).

169 403 U.S. 15 (1971).

170 *Id.* at 16.

what they regard as a suitable level of discourse within the body politic."[171]

First, verbal tumult, discord, and offensive utterances are in truth only the necessary side effects of removing governmental restraints from public discussion in order that the decision as to what ideas and emotions shall be voiced, and how they shall be voiced, shall be put in the hands of each of us individually, in the faith that experience in the use of such freedom to choose will ultimately produce a more capable citizenry and more perfect polity. "No other approach would comport with the premise of individual dignity and choice upon which our political system rests."[172] Second, the state can at best strike only at the most extremely offensive words, yet it can offer no principled distinction between words it must tolerate and those it would forbid.[173] Third, speakers often choose vulgarities to convey otherwise inexpressible emotions. The communication of emotions is as important a part of public discourse as the explication of intellectual ideas. Sometimes no other words quite serve the purpose.[174]

Later cases place more reliance upon the doctrine of overbreadth or the duty of a policeman to suffer verbal abuse, but upon one ground or another they reverse convictions for such utterances as "white son of a bitch, I'll kill you"[175] and "m ___ f___ fascist pig cops"[176] or calling the prosecution witness "chickenshit" during a prosecution for assault and battery.[177] Only the diversity of opinion among the Justices and the frequency of dissent suggest that the "fighting words" doctrine of *Chaplinsky v. New Hampshire*[178] may not be entirely dead.

The "dirty words" cases test the limits of a state's power to protect the sensibilities and thus the private spiritual life of

---

[171] *Id.* at 23.
[172] *Id.* at 24–25.
[173] *Id.* at 25–26.
[174] *Id.* at 26.
[175] Gooding v. Wilson, 405 U.S. 518 (1972).
[176] Brown v. Oklahoma, 408 U.S. 914 (1972).
[177] Eaton v. City of Tulsa, 415 U.S. 697 (1974).
[178] 315 U.S. 568 (1942).

unconsenting listeners or observers. The interest is akin to that of the private citizen subjected to unwanted publicity. Earlier decisions grant a measure of protection to citizens' privacy interests in nonpublic places.[179] The task of accommodation in public places is singularly difficult because gross offense to the sensibilities usually results only from certain classes of words or symbols, most notably the sexual, scatological, or sacrilegious. To assert that no time and place restrictions against the communication of particular ideas is ever constitutional unless the demanding test otherwise applicable to censorship is satisfied implies that the state is powerless to protect the sensibilities of an unconsenting audience against grossly offensive expression. Conversely, any restriction upon expression narrowly tailored to protect sensibility against gross assault is almost by definition tied to content and thus subject to attack as discriminatory, even when the restraint is limited in time or place.

B. Regulation Keyed to Content

Even though a limitation confined to time, place, or manner of expression obviously does less violence to the underlying values of the first amendment than a total prohibition upon the expression of specific ideas or information, the strong policy against governmental censorship of the content of communications requires that both restrictions and prohibitions be judged by much the same test, subject to exceptions based upon the special character of the forum.[180] The state has no greater power to punish speeches delivered between 6 p.m.

---

[179] See, e.g., Rowan v. United States Post Office Dep't, 397 U.S. 728 (1970); Breard v. Alexandria, 341 U.S. 622 (1951).

[180] See also Ely, Flag Desecration: A Case Study in the Roles of Categorization and Balancing in First Amendment Analysis, 88 HARV. L. REV. 1482, 1498 (1975). In Tinker v. Des Moines Indep. Community School Dist., 393 U.S. 503, 514 (1969), the Warren Court held students could not be suspended for wearing black armbands protesting the Vietnam War, but stated that school officials may prohibit speech they forecast will lead to "substantial disruption of or material interference with school activities."

and 10 p.m. advocating the overthrow of the government by force and violence than it has to prohibit the advocacy entirely.

A corollary principle strikes down a regulation of time, place, or manner of expression that discriminates between subjects of expression. *Police Department v. Mosley*,[181] for example, affirmed a decree enjoining enforcement of a municipal ordinance that forbade all picketing near school buildings during school hours except "the peaceful picketing of any school involved in a labor dispute."[182] Last Term, *Carey v. Brown*[183] invalidated an Illinois statute declaring it "unlawful to picket before or about the residence or dwelling of any person" because of an exception for the "peaceful picketing of a place of employment involved in a labor dispute."

In *Erznoznik v. City of Jacksonville*,[184] the Court ruled invalid on its face an ordinance prohibiting the exhibition of motion pictures displaying "the human male or female bare buttocks, human female bare breasts, or human bare pubic areas," upon a screen "visible from any public street or public place."[185]

A State or municipality may protect individual privacy by enacting reasonable time, place, and manner regulations applicable to all speech irrespective of content. But when the government, acting as censor, undertakes selectively to shield the public from some kinds of speech on the ground that they are more offensive than others, the First Amendment strictly limits its power.[186]

Perhaps the doctrine invoked is to be applied with caution. *Erznoznik* presses the doctrine condemning selective regulation to a questionable extreme. Only grossly offensive messages assault the sensibilities of unconsenting hearers or viewers. To forbid more would render a statute overbroad. To

---

[181] 408 U.S. 92 (1972).
[182] 408 U.S. at 94 n.2 (quoting CHICAGO MUNICIPAL CODE ch. 193-1 (i)).
[183] 100 S. Ct. 2286 (1980).
[184] 422 U.S. 205 (1975).
[185] *Id.* at 207.
[186] *Id.* at 209 (citations omitted).

forbid none, however offensive, would leave the sensibilities
unprotected. It seems unlikely that the Court intended to give
the states only this Hobson's choice. A display of public nudity
by twenty pickets in Harvard Square protesting a sales tax on
clothes or a sexual orgy on Cambridge Common advocating
the abolition of marriage might qualify as symbolic speech but
one suspects that the first amendment does not bar the state
from shielding the public from this form of speech on the
ground that it is more offensive than others. The *Erznoznik*
decision can readily be explained by the breadth of the prohibition against any display of nudity and the degree of interference with the management of drive-in theaters.

The Burger Court's otherwise consistent practice of invalidating any general regulation of the time, place, or manner
of expression keyed to content was sharply broken in *Young
v. American Mini Theatres, Inc.*[187] Justice Stevens' plurality
opinion, as explained above,[188] justified the departure with
the candid explanation that near-to-pornographic material is
only second-class speech. Justice Powell, to whom this rationale was unacceptable, sought to distinguish his *Erznoznik* opinion upon the ground that the Detroit ordinance "affects expression only incidentally and in furtherance of governmental
interests wholly unrelated to the regulation of expression."[189]
The distinction seems questionable unless the Jacksonville ordinance effectively imposed a total ban upon the exhibition of
nudity at drive-in theaters. Otherwise, both the Jacksonville
and Detroit ordinances regulated only the location or other
physical conditions under which the films could be exhibited,
even though both also tied regulation to content and both were
adopted because the lawmaking authorities believed objection-
able consequences to flow from its unregulated expression.

FCC v. Pacifica Foundation[190] illustrates the analytical
complexity of the problem and the delicacy of the judgment

---

[187] 427 U.S. 50 (1976); *see* p. 34 *supra*.
[188] *See* pp. 34–35 *supra*.
[189] 427 U.S. at 84 (Powell, J., concurring)
[190] 438 U.S. 726 (1978).

required when the first amendment interest in a virtually absolute barrier to government regulation of the content of speech
conflicts with the interest of individuals in avoiding indecent
forms of expression. The FCC had sustained a complaint
against a radio station for broadcasting at two o'clock on a
Tuesday afternoon the recording of a twelve-minute mono-
logue entitled "Filthy Words," which a satirical humorist had
previously delivered in a theater to the great amusement of the
audience. The words lived up to their billing. In upholding
the FCC order against the claim that the broadcast was protected by the first amendment, the plurality and concurring
Justices stressed the unusual combination of particular circumstances, each of which had been thought to call, in other
circumstances, for modification of the usual prohibition against
content regulation: (1) the unique character of broadcasting;[191]
(2) the intrusion of the broadcast into the homes of an initially
unconsenting audience, "the one place where people ordinarily
have the right not to be assaulted by uninvited and offensive
sights and sounds";[192] (3) the impact upon children;[193] and (4)
the FCC's emphasis upon channeling such broadcasts into
hours when the fewest unsupervised children would be exposed, which made it possible to view the order as one limiting
only the time of expression.[194] Justice Stevens, joined by the
Chief Justice and Justice Rehnquist, put much emphasis upon
the plurality opinion in *American Mini Theatres*, holding that
the explicitly sexual or scatological is only second-class
speech.[195] Justices Powell and Blackmun, whose votes were
necessary to make up the five-member majority, rejected "the

---

[191] *See* Red Lion Broadcasting Co. v. FCC, 395 U.S. 367 (1969).

[192] 438 U.S. at 759 (Powell, J., concurring in part and in the judgment); *cf.* Rowan
v. United States Post Office Dep't, 397 U.S. 728, 736–38 (1970) (upholding federal
statute under which a person may prevent "sexually provocative" matter from being
mailed to his home).

[193] *Cf.* Ginsberg v. New York, 390 U.S. 629, 637 (1968) (minors have "a more
restricted right than that assured to adults to judge and determine for themselves
what 'sex material' they may read and see").

[194] 438 U.S. at 750; *id.* at 757 (Powell, J., concurring in part and in the judgment).

[195] 438 U.S. at 744–48 (opinion of Stevens, J.).

theory that the Justices of this Court are free generally to decide on the basis of its content which speech protected by the First Amendment is most 'valuable' and hence deserving of the most protection, and which is less 'valuable' and hence deserving of less protection."[196]

FCC v. Pacifica Foundation may come to be viewed as a narrow, highly particular decision pushing a number of doctrinal exceptions to first amendment principles to their limits because the exceptions conjoin. Like other decisions relying upon the coincidence of a number of borderline exceptions, it is susceptible of use as a precedent for the expansion of each.

C. Right to a Forum

Some Justices and commentators have viewed the doctrines discussed in the two Sections of this essay immediately above as collectively sufficient to establish a first amendment right to a public forum.[197] The concept seems to assume that there are some places in which expression may not be limited — indeed that an appropriate forum must be provided to would-be speakers — provided that the speakers do not seriously interfere with other public uses. At a minimum it implies a presumption that any restriction upon expression in the public forum is unjustified.

The difference in approach is illustrated by the majority and concurring opinions in *Hynes v. Mayor & Council*.[198] The Borough of Oradell had enacted an ordinance prohibiting peddlers and other solicitors from canvassing door-to-door without a permit from the chief of police. The challenge was to an ordinance prohibiting house-to-house canvassing for "a recognized charitable cause, or . . . political campaign or cause" without written notice to the police department "for identification only."[199] The opinion of the Court by Chief

---

[196] *Id.* at 761 (Powell, J., concurring in part and in the judgment).

[197] *E.g.*, L. TRIBE, AMERICAN CONSTITUTIONAL LAW § 12-21 (1978); G. GUNTHER, CONSTITUTIONAL LAW 1195–200, 1215–19 (10th ed. 1980).

[198] 425 U.S. 610 (1976).

[199] *Id.* at 612–13.

Justice Burger held the second ordinance unconstitutionally vague because its coverage was unclear and because it did not sufficiently specify what was necessary for compliance. Justices Brennan and Marshall concurred in that portion of the opinion of the Court, but they specifically disagreed with a portion of the Chief Justice's opinion asserting "a municipality's power to protect its citizens from crime and undue annoyance by regulating soliciting and canvassing."[200] They went further to declare that the first amendment secures the right to canvass door-to-door in anonymity.[201]

The substantive issue aside, this unnecessary division of opinion, like others among members of the Burger Court,[202] will give concern to those who believe in the wisdom of Chief Justice Marshall's determination that the Court should whenever possible speak with one voice.[203] Eight Justices adjudged the Oradell ordinance void for vagueness. Surely, it was possible to develop one opinion explaining that conclusion and saying no more.

The very recent opinion of the Court in *Village of Schaumburg v. Citizens for a Better Environment*[204] puts more emphasis than *Hynes v. Mayor & Council* upon the first amendment interests in door-to-door solicitation in holding unconstitutional an ordinance barring door-to-door and street solicitation by charitable organizations using less than seventy-five percent of their receipts for "charitable purposes" (excluding the expenses of solicitation), but the decision was placed upon the ground that the regulation was overbroad. The decision necessarily holds that canvassing for contributions for a charitable or political cause is an activity entitled to some degree of protection under the first amendment and necessarily condemns un-

---

[200] *Id.* at 616–17.

[201] *Id.* at 623–30 (Brennan, J., concurring in part).

[202] *See* pp. 29–31 *supra.*

[203] President Jefferson ascribed the practice to Chief Justice Marshall, but Charles Warren concluded that the change from the practice of seriatim opinions occurred before Marshall became Chief Justice. 1 C. WARREN, THE SUPREME COURT IN UNITED STATES HISTORY 653–54 (rev. ed. 1926).

[204] 444 U.S. 620 (1980).

justified discrimination against one form of this activity. Yet because the Village of Schaumburg did permit other door-to-door activity, this decision, like all that preceded it, stops short of upholding a general right of access to a public forum.[205]

Efforts to establish a first amendment right of access to government-owned places not generally available for sundry forms of public expression have uniformly failed.[206] Furthermore, although the opinions leave room for the view that the government's power to regulate expression in areas such as military bases is less than absolute, the decisions permit content-based distinctions that the first amendment would proscribe if the communication were on the streets or in a park or other open and public locations.[207] The most difficult of these cases upheld the power of a municipality to exclude political advertising from the space that it leased to other advertisers on the public transit system.[208] The contrast between this last group of cases and those dealing with streets, parks, and public auditoriums indicates that even if the state theoretically has no duty to supply forums for public demonstration or discussion, the first amendment safeguards do extend to the forums conventionally open to the public with a rigor not applicable to other locations.

After some vacillation,[209] the Court rejected efforts to ex-

---

[205] Professor Tribe cites Southeastern Promotions, Ltd. v. Conrad, 420 U.S. 546 (1975), as establishing a right to a public forum because the Court found that the city of Chattanooga violated the first amendment rights of the producers in refusing to allow a performance of the rock musical *Hair* in the municipal theater. L. TRIBE, *supra* note 197, § 12-21, at 689 n.4. As I read the opinion, the violation was in the city's failure to follow the procedural requirements of Freedman v. Maryland, 380 U.S. 51 (1965), but that holding probably implies that the producer had a first amendment right not to be denied access arbitrarily. Once again, however, the case is one of discrimination tied to content; other producers were voluntarily granted access to the auditorium.

[206] Brown v. Glines, 444 U.S. 348 (1980); Greer v. Spock, 424 U.S. 828 (1976); Lehman v. City of Shaker Heights, 418 U.S. 298 (1974); Adderley v. Florida, 385 U.S. 39 (1966).

[207] *See* pp. 52–53 *supra*.

[208] Lehman v. City of Shaker Heights, 418 U.S. 298 (1974).

[209] Lloyd Corp. v. Tanner, 407 U.S. 551 (1972); Central Hardware Co. v. NLRB,

pand the doctrine of *Marsh v. Alabama*[210] in order to create a first amendment right to use privately owned retail malls and shopping centers for picketing, leafletting, and other public appeals.[211] The retail mall and shopping center serves much the same public functions as Main Street and the public square. Without a right of access, the isolation of businesses and workers in industrial parks and migrant labor camps cuts off familiar methods of communication. Now that the effort to solve these problems under the first amendment has foundered for lack of "state action," new and better solutions are being developed under the National Labor Relations Act[212] and sundry state laws.[213] In *PruneYard Shopping Center v. Robins*[214] the Court ruled that a state has the power to require a privately owned shopping center to grant access to members of the public soliciting signatures to a political petition. Such methods of accommodating the law of trespass to modern conditions seem much preferable to abandonment of the distinction between state and private activity.

III. EXPRESSIVE CONDUCT

The bold line that the Burger Court has drawn between restrictions upon publication and regulation of the time, place,

---

407 U.S. 539 (1972); Food Employees Local 590 v. Logan Valley Plaza, Inc., 391 U.S. 308 (1968).

[210] 326 U.S. 501 (1946) (business corporation maintaining a company town may not exclude Jehovah's Witnesses from seeking converts on street open to public).

[211] Hudgens v. NLRB, 424 U.S. 507 (1976).

[212] *E.g.*, Scott Hudgens, 230 N.L.R.B. 414 (1977); Holland Rantos Co., 234 N.L.R.B. 726, *enforced*, 583 F.2d 100 (3d Cir. 1978).

[213] *See, e.g.*, Sears, Roebuck & Co. v. San Diego County Dist. Council of Carpenters, 25 Cal. 3d 317, 324–25, 599 P.2d 676, 681 (1979) (act limiting jurisdiction of superior court to enjoin peaceful picketing if it "occurs in 'any . . . place where any person or persons may lawfully be,'") (quoting CAL. CIV. PROC. CODE § 527.3(b)(1) (West 1978)). The common law recognizes a variety of privileges to enter upon real estate. *See, e.g.*, W. PROSSER, HANDBOOK OF THE LAW OF TORTS §§ 23–27 (4th ed. 1971). It should be flexible enough to adjust to the need for access for the purpose of communication.

[214] 100 S. Ct. 2035 (1980), *discussed in The Supreme Court, 1979 Term*, 94 HARV. L. REV. 75, 169–78 (1980).

or manner of expression tied to content, on the one hand, and regulation of time, place, or manner of expression regardless of content, on the other hand, reflects the difference between the state's usually impermissible effort to suppress "harmful" information, ideas, or emotions and the state's often justifiable desire to secure other interests against interference from the noise and the physical intrusions that accompany speech, regardless of the information, ideas, or emotions expressed. Inquiry into the character of the danger with which the regulation is concerned offers a constructive solution to the vexing problem of expressive conduct.[215] Even the utterance of words and distribution of leaflets involve some degree of physical activity. Burning a tyrant in effigy is pure conduct, but it may communicate more than a speech. The speech/conduct distinction is too superficial to be useful. All three forms of expression should be protected against suppression for their "dangerous" ideas. All three may be subject to a degree of regulation based upon the nonideological consequences of the particular form of activity.

The decision in *Spence v. Washington* is consistent with this approach even though the opinion does not adopt it.[216] Spence, a university student, attached a peace symbol to a flag of the United States and hung the flag upside down from the window of his apartment on private property shortly after the invasion of Cambodia and the shooting at Kent State. There was not the slightest tendency to provoke a breach of the peace. Spence was prosecuted and convicted under a state statute making it a crime to "place . . . any . . . design . . . upon any flag" of the United States or to exhibit a flag upon which a design had been fixed.[217] There was general agreement that Spence was engaged in a form of communication

---

[215] *See generally* Ely, *supra* note 180.

[216] 418 U.S. 405 (1974) (per curiam). Earlier the Court had adopted this approach in United States v. O'Brien, 391 U.S. 367 (1968), holding that even if burning a draft card is sufficiently communicative to bring into play the first amendment, that activity may be punished in order to secure the government's interest in requiring persons subject to selective service to keep such cards in their possession.

[217] 418 U.S. at 407.

bringing into play the first amendment. The Supreme Court of Washington in affirming the conviction had held that the state's interest in preserving the symbolic integrity of the flag is sufficiently important to justify prohibiting its use to convey other messages. The U.S. Supreme Court reversed, 5–4, but the per curiam opinion seeks to diffuse rather than meet the rationale below. After taxing both the court below and their dissenting colleagues of failing to define the "interest in preserving the flag as an unalloyed symbol of our country,"[218] the majority suggested that the state might have two interests in prohibiting the display of a flag to which another design has been affixed: (1) the interest in preventing misunderstanding concerning "governmental endorsement"; (2) the interest in preserving the "uniquely universal character" of the flag as a symbol.[219] Because there was neither danger of misunderstanding nor permanent injury to the physical integrity of the flag, the Court held that the conviction must be reversed.

It is difficult to explain both the majority's studied refusal to understand what the court below meant by the "interest in preserving the flag as an unalloyed symbol of our country"[220] and its persistence in dealing only with the physical integrity of the particular flag. The point made by the court below and by the dissent is plain enough. For most of the American people the flag symbolizes not whatever anyone wishes to make of it but our patriotism, our loyalty, our pride and unity as a nation. Not everyone views the flag in that fashion, but as a whole this is our view, and the Washington statute embodied it. There is an interest in perpetuating a symbol capable of evoking such emotions. The flag's capacity to evoke them is eroded by putting it to other uses even if the flag is not physically disfigured. The interest, in the view of the dissent, is appropriate for governmental protection and outweighs the

---

[218] *Id.* at 412.

[219] "It might be said that we all draw something from our national symbol, for it is capable of conveying simultaneously a spectrum of meanings. If it may be destroyed or permanently disfigured, it could be argued that it will lose its capability of mirroring the sentiments of all who view it." *Id.* at 412–13.

[220] *Id.* at 412.

interest in using the flag for communicating other ideas.[221]
The per curiam opinion seems to reject the argument but never
faces it expressly.[222] Perhaps the omission results from the
majority's inability to agree upon a rationale. In my opinion
the short and correct answer would have been that, except in
cases presenting the kind of clear and present danger recognized by Justice Brandeis,[223] a state may never punish either
the expression of political ideas or the choice of symbols because of their ideological consequences.

IV. REGULATION OF CONDUCT AFFECTING PUBLICATION

Many regulatory laws of general applicability may affect
the ability of a publisher to circulate information, argument,
or literary or artistic material, even though there is neither
discrimination nor direct regulation of the content, time, place,
or manner of expression. To require journalists to comply
with the legal obligations imposed upon the general body of
citizens may impair their ability to gather and publish news.
Stressing the extraordinary importance of their function o.
gathering and distributing the information required by a self-
governing people, newspaper publishers and reporters often
invoke the first amendment in an effort to establish a special
privilege that would exempt them from some law of general
applicability. Thus, in 1937, the Associated Press unsuccessfully claimed that application of the National Labor Relations
Act to its employment of reporters and editors would violate
the first amendment.[224] The American Newspaper Publishers
Association supported prolonged but ultimately unsuccessful
litigation challenging the constitutionality of requiring newspapers to comply with the minimum wage and overtime restrictions applicable to other employment in the production of

---

[221] *Id.* at 416–17 (Rehnquist, J., dissenting).
[222] 418 U.S. at 413–14.
[223] Whitney v. California, 274 U.S. 357, 373–78 (1927) (Brandeis, J., concurring).
[224] Associated Press v. NLRB, 301 U.S. 103, 130–33 (1937).

goods for interstate commerce.[225] *Associated Press v. United States*[226] rejected an assertion that the first amendment precludes application of the Sherman Act to an organization gathering and disseminating news.

Several analogous but more appealing claims to this kind of privilege were pressed by the media during the 1970's. Every person has a duty, subject to rare exceptions, to give evidence required in the administration of justice.[227] This principle was the foundation of the order requiring President Nixon to produce the Watergate tapes.[228] In *Branzburg v. Hayes*,[229] a newspaper reporter refused to answer a grand jury's questions concerning illegal drug traffic that he had personally observed, claiming that the first amendment gives a reporter freedom not to disclose sources of information and to decide how much he will disclose of what he has learned. The reporter argued that if a journalist is forced to reveal in court or before a grand jury information given in confidence, then particular sources of information will dry up, "all to the detriment of the free flow of information protected by the First Amendment."[230] The claimed constitutional privilege had not been recognized previously.[231] At its core the issue requires balancing any effects of denying the privilege upon the flow of information important to the public against the effects of granting it upon the administration of justice. A bare majority of the Supreme Court adhered to the existing law and, putting the needs of the administration of justice first, denied the privilege. Although the opinion of the Court seems rather

---

[225] The claim was finally rejected in Oklahoma Press Publishing Co. v. Walling, 327 U.S. 186, 192–94 (1946).

[226] 326 U.S. 1 (1945).

[227] 8 J. WIGMORE, EVIDENCE § 2192 (J. McNaughton rev. 1961); 4 THE WORKS OF JEREMY BENTHAM 320–21 (J. Bowring ed. 1843).

[228] United States v. Nixon, 418 U.S. 683, 708–09 (1974).

[229] 408 U.S. 665 (1972).

[230] *Id.* at 680.

[231] *See* Garland v. Torre, 259 F.2d 545 (2d Cir.), *cert. denied*, 358 U.S. 910 (1958); Brewster v. Boston Herald-Traveler Corp., 20 F.R.D. 416 (D. Mass. 1957); *In re* Goodfader's Appeal, 45 Hawaii 317, 367 P.2d 472 (1961).

plainly to hold that a reporter has "no First Amendment privilege to refuse to answer the relevant and material questions asked during a good-faith grand jury investigation,"[232] Justice Powell found it possible both to concur in that general holding and to assert that a court should balance "these vital constitutional and societal interests on a case-by-case basis."[233] The resulting ambiguity has yet to be clarified.

The press has been bitterly critical of *Branzburg v. Hayes*.[234] The fairness of the criticism depends upon the same question of fact as the decision itself: To what extent will the obligation to give testimony identifying confidential sources when required in the administration of justice deprive the public of information important to the citizens' ability to govern themselves? Editors and reporters, who should know more about the subject than any other group, often assert with much conviction that the loss will be great, but there is room to ask whether they have analyzed their observations with both care and detachment.[235] Supreme Court Justices, on the other hand, have little basis for anything more than intelligent speculation about the underlying question of fact. With plausible arguments on both sides, perhaps the final constitutional judgment should turn on whether the press should bear the burden of persuasion when it claims that the first amendment gives it a special exemption not to comply with an important legal obligation imposed upon others in society, because compliance will indirectly interfere with gathering and publishing the news.[236] To put this burden upon a speaker, publisher, or

---

[232] 408 U.S. at 708.

[233] *Id.* at 710.

[234] *See* Comment, *The Newsman's Privilege after* Branzburg v. Hayes: *Whither Now?*, 64 J. CRIM. L.C. & P.S. 218, 218 n.3 (1973).

[235] At least two difficulties arise in appraising whatever data are obtainable. First, the question of what information any particular informant would withhold under a given rule of law will usually be hypothetical. Second, the need to give a generally phrased promise of confidentiality is scarcely proof of the need to give assurance that the reporter cannot even be required to make disclosure under subpoena.

[236] This problem illustrates once again the frequency with which constitutional issues reduce themselves to questions of fact. In cases like *Branzburg v. Hayes*, the question of fact will generally be resolved by some judicial tribunal because no

demonstrator invoking the first amendment to challenge a direct restriction upon expression or a regulation discriminating against speech would be intolerable, but it may be more acceptable when the effects upon speech are indirect and the claim is for a constitutional exemption from a general legal duty.[237] In the *Branzburg* situation, moreover, the press enjoys considerable opportunity to persuade legislatures, judges, and prosecutors of the necessity for recognition of a larger testimonial privilege than the first amendment requires.[238]

The press also unsuccessfully sought special exemption from the general rules of pretrial discovery in *Herbert v. Lando*.[239] The action was brought by a public figure to recover damages for defamation. The plaintiff, in order to prevail, would be required to prove that the defendants had published the false and defamatory statement either knowing it to be false or with conscious indifference to its possible untruth.[240] Accordingly, plaintiff's counsel sought during pretrial discovery to interrogate the defendants, their colleagues,

---

legislative body will have expressed its conclusion. There is difficulty not only in determining how to assign the burden of persuasion, *see* pp. 36–37 *supra*, but also in prescribing the method by which the relevant data should be brought before a court.

[237] It can be argued that this suggestion is inconsistent with such cases as Gibson v. Florida Legislative Investigation Comm., 372 U.S. 539 (1963), and DeGregory v. Attorney Gen., 383 U.S. 825 (1966). *See* Branzburg v. Hayes, 408 U.S. 665, 738–43 (1972) (Stewart, J., dissenting). In these cases, however, the legislative or executive body was engaged in a broad-scale investigation into political activity, thus making the issue more nearly one of whether direct sanctions against the exercise of first amendment liberties were justified by an important public purpose.

[238] The U.S. Department of Justice has adopted a stringent rule restricting the issuance of subpoenas addressed to journalists. 28 C.F.R. § 50.10 (1979); United States Attorneys' Manual § 1-5.410 (1980). A number of states adopted or strengthened existing shield laws following the decision in *Branzburg v. Hayes*. *E.g.*, N.Y. CIV. RIGHTS LAW § 79-h (McKinney 1976); OR. REV. STAT. §§ 44.520, .530 (1979). A case involving the constitutionality of a shield law when the defendant charged with a major criminal offense seeks a reporter's testimony as necessary to the preservation of his constitutional right to a fair trial reached the New Jersey Supreme Court in *In re* Farber, 78 N.J. 259, 394 A.2d 330 (1978), but certiorari was refused, 439 U.S. 997 (1978).

[239] 441 U.S. 153 (1979).

[240] *See* pp. 14–19 *supra*.

and editors about their beliefs and conferences while the story
was being prepared for publication. Because the defendants'
state of mind was a critical issue, most of the questions were
plainly material and necessary under the general rules of discovery.[241] Defendants claimed an exception because the financial burden of such discovery proceedings might deter
publication of possible defamatory statements and because
editorial conferences should be kept confidential in order to
encourage free editorial discussion.[242]

It is hardly surprising that no Justice fully accepted the
argument.[243] Pretrial discovery often imposes a heavy financial burden, but the burdens on publishers and broadcasters
seem neither greater nor less than those on other litigants. If
the *New York Times* rule sufficiently protects first amendment
interests, there should be no procedural discrimination against
plaintiffs seeking to pursue the customary procedural steps for
proving a case. The affront felt by editors and reporters when
sharply questioned about their thoughts and emotions while
preparing a story is readily understandable, but it too appears
to be a consequence of the substantive law that attaches significance to an actor's state of mind.[244]

Zurcher v. Stanford Daily[245] refused to give the press special immunity from search warrants issued by a judicial mag-
istrate upon a showing of probable cause to believe that the
files of a student newspaper contained pictures that would be
useful evidence in identifying the leaders of a riotous demonstration who had committed felonious assaults upon police
officers. Although the novelty of the question precludes doctrinal criticism, the wisdom of the Court's judgment seems

---

[241] *See* 441 U.S. at 157.

[242] 441 U.S. at 171, 173, 175-77.

[243] Justice Marshall in a dissenting opinion accepted the defendant's argument that
editorial conferences should be privileged. *Id.* at 204-06. Justice Brennan would
have granted editorial communications a privilege defeasible upon a prima facie
showing that the publication was false and defamatory. *Id.* at 180-89 (opinion
dissenting in part).

[244] 441 U.S. at 160, 172.

[245] 436 U.S. 547 (1978).

questionable. In 1967, *Warden v. Hayden*[246] wrought a profound change in fourth amendment law by holding that a search warrant may issue not only for contraband, weapons, and the fruits of crime, but also, contrary to the previous general understanding, for evidence. There is much force to Justice Stevens' argument that the expansion of the uses of search warrants should be accompanied by stronger safeguards for the reputation and privacy of the persons whose premises are subjected to a search for evidence.[247] In this instance, moreover, the press appears to be on pretty solid ground when it argues that it is subject to peculiar risks of harassment. Investigative reporting and coverage of newsworthy events, coupled with the absence of any testimonial privilege, make a newspaper's premises a much more likely source of evidence than the premises of ordinary citizens or businesses. In addition, the police, prosecutors, and other officials are under stronger temptation to harass their critics, especially small but shrill voices on the fringe of "responsible opinion." In a period of heightened emotion there would be increased danger of raids upon their premises, with the authorities ostensibly searching for evidence but actually looking for whatever weapon of embarrassment may turn up. The Burger Court's attachment to law enforcement thus seems to me to have dulled unduly its sensitivity to the threat posed here to freedom of expression. Congress, being more sensitive to the dangers of abuse, recently restricted severely the issuance of such warrants for newspaper searches.[248]

Taken as a whole, this group of cases emphasizes the contrast between the strong bulwark provided by the first amendment against direct suppression or regulation of publication or expression and the kind of factual inquiry and balancing necessary when a special privilege is sought because of the indirect effects of a generally valid legal obligation.

---

[246] 387 U.S. 294 (1967).

[247] 436 U.S. at 577–83 (Stevens, J., dissenting). Justices Stewart and Marshall, dissenting, invoked the first amendment. 436 U.S. at 570–77. Justice Brennan did not participate.

[248] *See* N.Y. Times, Oct. 15, 1980, at A28, col. 4.

V. FINANCING POLITICAL CAMPAIGNS[249]

Two major first amendment decisions of the past decade deal with the extent and limits of legislative power to regulate the financing of political campaigns: *Buckley v. Valeo*[250] and *First National Bank v. Bellotti.*[251] The questions were novel; the decisions leave many questions unanswered; but upon the broadest interpretation the cases can be read to create under the first amendment a broad and virtually unqualified individual, associational right to spend unlimited sums of money in political campaigns. The broad interpretations and perhaps even the rationale of the decisions will surely be challenged by those who fear that the rulings do more to enhance the political power of money than to promote the goals of the first amendment.

Buckley v. Valeo grew out of a many-faceted challenge to the Federal Election Campaign Act Amendments of 1974.[252] The Amendments reflected deep public and congressional concern about the poisonous effect of large campaign contributions upon the entire political system. By 1974 it was apparent that advertising campaigns based upon the use of television and other modern media of mass communications had transformed American politics and also enormously increased the role of money.[253]

---

[249] The reader should understand that although I have tried to make a fair presentation of the decisions and issues discussed in this Part, I write it without scholarly detachment. My views are undoubtedly affected by my involvement with the issues as counsel for amici curiae in Buckley v. Valeo, 424 U.S. 1 (1976), and by my position as chairman of the Governing Board of Common Cause, an organization that lobbies for restrictions upon the size of political election campaign contributions, and for the substitution of public funds.

[250] 424 U.S. 1 (1976).

[251] 435 U.S. 765 (1978).

[252] Pub. L. No. 93-443, 88 Stat. 1263 (1974) (current version at 2 U.S.C. §§ 431–455 (1976).

[253] Spending in presidential elections rose dramatically:

1952 — $11.6 million
1960 — 19.9 million
1968 — 44.2 million
1972 — 83   million

Given the extraordinary expenditures, it is hardly surprising that candidates increasingly turned to those whose personal ambitions, business affairs, or organized economic interests were directly and substantially affected by government decisions that the successful candidate could influence. Government had become the chief buyer of goods, the largest employer, the dispenser of subsidies through direct benefit or tax advantage, the regulator and manager of the economy, and the adjuster of many conflicts among economic interests. As the role of money rose, so increased the obligation that the successful candidate owed to the large contributors who supplied the supposed means of victory. Senator Russell Long once observed: "When you are talking in terms of large campaign contributions . . . the distinction between a campaign contribution and a bribe is almost a hair's line difference."[254]

Public distrust, cynicism, and alienation were generated by the coincidence of contribution and receipt of governmental

---

In constant dollars, for every $1 spent in 1952, almost $3 was spent in 1968, and $4.53 in 1972. Similarly, for every $100 spent by presidential candidates in 1962, $521 was spent in 1974 — a fivefold increase without adjustment for inflation, a threefold increase even in constant dollars. Amici Curiae Brief of Senators Hugh Scott and Edward M. Kennedy at 35, Buckley v. Valeo, 424 U.S. 1 (1976).

[254] *Hearings on S. 3496, Amendment No. 732, S. 2006, S. 2965, and S. 3014 Before the Senate Comm. on Finance*, 89th Cong., 2d Sess. 78 (1966). One contributor of $100,000 during the 1972 election campaign testified that he had no strong desire to help reelect the President, but that he did hope that his contribution would secure the lifting of an order suspending him from bidding on government construction contracts. *Hearings Before the Senate Select Comm. on Presidential Campaign Activities*, 93d Cong., 1st Sess. 5336–37 (1973) (testimony of John J. Priestes). Other businessmen testified that they were moved by fear that their competitors would fare better than they in dealing with government agencies, unless they matched their rivals' contributions. *Id.* at 5495, 5514 (testimony of George Spater, former Chairman and Chief Executive of American Airlines). An executive explained, "I think all we were attempting to do was to assure ourselves of a forum to be heard. . . . [W]e felt we needed something that would be sort of a calling card, something that would get us in the door and would make our point of view heard." *Id.* at 5442 (testimony of Orin E. Atkins). Herbert Kalmbach, President Nixon's personal lawyer, testified, "[I]n return for that [$100,000] contribution it would be possible for me to arrange for several appointments with various people within the White House . . . ." *Id.* at 7583. FINAL REPORT OF THE SENATE SELECT COMM. ON PRESIDENTIAL CAMPAIGN ACTIVITIES, S. REP. NO. 981, 93d Cong., 2d Sess. 593 (1974).

benefit, even when there was no proof of a causal relation. In 1974, recollections were still vivid of the Milk Producers Association's pledge of $2,000,000 to President Nixon's campaign for reelection, given at the same time as the Nixon Administration granted an increase in the support price of milk;[255] of the approval of American Airlines' applications for profitable routes shortly after a large and unlawful corporate contribution to the party in power;[256] and of the settlement of antitrust litigation against International Telephone & Telegraph Corporation shortly after an ITT subsidiary agreed to underwrite a large portion of the expenses of the Republican Party's national convention.[257]

The 1974 FECA Amendments attempted massive changes in the financing of federal election campaigns. The amendments —

1. Required detailed reporting and disclosure of campaign contributions and expenditures;[258]

2. Prohibited individuals from contributing more than $1,000 to any one candidate in any one primary or general election;[259]

3. Put ceilings on the expenditure of personal or family funds;[260]

4. Placed ceilings on the aggregate expenditures that might be made by or on behalf of a candidate for federal office;[261]

5. Forbade any person to expend more than $1,000 in "advocating the election or defeat" of "a clearly identified can-

---

[255] See Statement of Information, Political Contributions by Milk Producers Cooperatives: The 1971 Milk Price Support Decision, Hearings Before the House Comm. on the Judiciary, 93d Cong., 2d Sess. bk. VI, pt. II (1979).

[256] See Statement of Information, Papers in Criminal Cases, Hearings Before the House Comm. on the Judiciary, 93d Cong., 2d Sess. app. II, at 203 (1979).

[257] See Statement of Information, Department of Justice/ITT Litigation, Hearings Before the House Comm. on the Judiciary, 93d Cong., 2d Sess. bk. V, pt. I (1979) (Richard Kleindienst nomination hearings).

[258] Pub. L. No. 93-443, tit. II, §§ 201–210, 88 Stat. 1272–89 (1974) (current version at 2 U.S.C. §§ 431–439, 441, 451–452, 490(a)–(c) (1976)).

[259] Pub. L. No. 93-443, tit. I, § 101(a), 88 Stat. 1263 (1974) (repealed 1976).

[260] Pub. L. No. 93-443, tit. I, § 101(b)(1), 88 Stat. 1266 (1974) (repealed 1976).

[261] Pub. L. No. 93-443, tit. I, § 101(a), 88 Stat. 1264 (1974) (repealed 1976).

didate" even though the expenditure was made without cε
sultation with the candidate or his agents;[262]

6. Provided for federal financing of presidential election
campaigns from a fund provided by voluntary individual contributions of one dollar checked off from the income tax. In
the primaries, each candidate who raised funds in excess of
$5,000 in each of twenty states (counting the first $250 of any
individual's contribution) was entitled to federal matching
funds, dollar for dollar, for contributions raised by the candidate (again counting only the first $250 of each contribu-
tor).[263]

During the general election each major party candidate is
entitled to receive an equal allowance under a formula yielding
each $29.4 million in 1980 on condition that he agree neither
to make expenditures nor to incur debts in excess of that sum.
A related section prohibits any political committee not authorized by the candidate from expending more than $1,000 in
support of the election of a candidate who has elected to
receive federal funds.[264]

Challenges were promptly launched against every significant provision in the statute and received expedited treatment
in the federal courts as provided for in the amendments.[265]
The result was a massive lawsuit presenting a multiplicity of
difficult constitutional questions based on hypothetical allega-
tions of what the plaintiffs might wish to do in some future
political campaign.[266]

---

[262] Pub. L. No. 93-443, tit. I, § 101(a), 88 Stat. 1265 (1974) (repealed 1976).

[263] Pub. L. No. 93-443, tit. IV, § 408(a)–(c), 88 Stat. 1297–303 (1974) (codified at I.R.C. §§ 9031–9042).

[264] Pub. L. No. 93-443, tit. IV, §§ 403–404, 88 Stat. 1291–94 (1974) (current version at I.R.C. §§ 6096, 9002–9012).

[265] Pub. L. No. 93-443, tit. II, § 208A (current version at 2 U.S.C. § 437h (1976)).

[266] Buckley v. Valeo, 387 F. Supp. 135 (D.D.C.), *remanded in part per curiam*, 519 F.2d 817 (D.C. Cir. 1975) (en banc), *questions certified*, (D.D.C. May 19, 1975) (Corcoran, J.), *certified questions answered*, 401 F. Supp. 1235 (D.D.C. 1975) (special three-judge panel), *aff'd*, 424 U.S. 1 (1976); Buckley v. Valeo, 387 F. Supp. 135 (D.D.C. 1975), *remanded in part per curiam*, 519 F.2d 817 (D.C. Cir. 1975) (en banc), *questions certified*, (D.D.C. May 19, 1975) (Corcoran, J.), *certified questions answered in parallel proceedings*, 519 F.2d 821 (D.C. Cir. 1975) (en banc), *aff'd in part and*

The Supreme Court held that the provision for funding
presidential election campaigns is, in general, a constitutional
exercise of federal power.[267] It also ruled that the elaborate
disclosure and reporting requirements violate no right of
speech, assembly, or privacy, except when an individual or
organization can show that disclosure will result in the kind
of focused and insistent intimidation, harassment or reprisal
proved in *NAACP v. Alabama ex rel. Patterson*.[268] The majority also sought to chart a constitutional distinction between
the ceilings upon expenditures, which were held to violate the
first amendment, and the ceilings upon contributions, which
were sustained. This is plainly the most difficult and important aspect of the case.

Counsel defending the expenditure ceilings had argued in
various forms the basic point best expressed by Paul A.
Freund: "[Those who make large expenditures for the mass
media] are operating vicariously through the power of their
purse, rather than through the power of their ideas, and . . .
I would scale that relatively lower in the hierarchy of First
Amendment values."[269] Conversely, the argument proceeded,
the principal evil with which the Congress was concerned
flowed from the nonspeech element, the money, and not as a
consequence of the ideas expressed. The principles discussed
earlier in this essay would lead from that predicate to the
conclusion that, although some first amendment protection
would extend to spending that supported speech, the expenditure regulation could be justified by showing that it served
a substantial public interest.[270]

The Court held that political expenditures are protected by
the first amendment as fully as speech itself:

---

rev'd in part, 424 U.S. 1 (1976). *See also* Leventhal, *Courts and Political Thickets*,
77 COLUM. L. REV. 345 (1977).

[267] Buckley v. Valeo, 424 U.S. 1 (1976).

[268] 357 U.S. 449 (1958).

[269] A. ROSENTHAL, FEDERAL REGULATION OF CAMPAIGN FINANCE 72–73 (1971)
(commentary by Paul Freund).

[270] *See* pp. 47–48, 59–60 *supra*.

didate" even though the expenditure was made without con-
sultation with the candidate or his agents;[262]

6. Provided for federal financing of presidential election
campaigns from a fund provided by voluntary individual contributions of one dollar checked off from the income tax. In
the primaries, each candidate who raised funds in excess of
$5,000 in each of twenty states (counting the first $250 of any
individual's contribution) was entitled to federal matching
funds, dollar for dollar, for contributions raised by the candidate (again counting only the first $250 of each contribu-
tor).[263]

During the general election each major party candidate is
entitled to receive an equal allowance under a formula yielding
each $29.4 million in 1980 on condition that he agree neither
to make expenditures nor to incur debts in excess of that sum.
A related section prohibits any political committee not authorized by the candidate from expending more than $1,000 in
support of the election of a candidate who has elected to
receive federal funds.[264]

Challenges were promptly launched against every significant provision in the statute and received expedited treatment
in the federal courts as provided for in the amendments.[265]
The result was a massive lawsuit presenting a multiplicity of
difficult constitutional questions based on hypothetical allega-
tions of what the plaintiffs might wish to do in some future
political campaign.[266]

---

[262] Pub. L. No. 93-443, tit. I, § 101(a), 88 Stat. 1265 (1974) (repealed 1976).

[263] Pub. L. No. 93-443, tit. IV, § 408(a)–(c), 88 Stat. 1297–303 (1974) (codified at
I.R.C. §§ 9031–9042).

[264] Pub. L. No. 93-443, tit. IV, §§ 403–404, 88 Stat. 1291–94 (1974) (current
version at I.R.C. §§ 6096, 9002–9012).

[265] Pub. L. No. 93-443, tit. II, § 208A (current version at 2 U.S.C. § 437h (1976)).

[266] Buckley v. Valeo, 387 F. Supp. 135 (D.D.C.), *remanded in part per curiam*,
519 F.2d 817 (D.C. Cir. 1975) (en banc), *questions certified*, (D.D.C. May 19, 1975)
(Corcoran, J.), *certified questions answered*, 401 F. Supp. 1235 (D.D.C. 1975) (special
three-judge panel), *aff'd*, 424 U.S. 1 (1976); Buckley v. Valeo, 387 F. Supp. 135
(D.D.C. 1975), *remanded in part per curiam*, 519 F.2d 817 (D.C. Cir. 1975) (en banc),
questions certified, (D.D.C. May 19, 1975) (Corcoran, J.), *certified questions answered
in parallel proceedings*, 519 F.2d 821 (D.C. Cir. 1975) (en banc), *aff'd in part and*

The Supreme Court held that the provision for funding presidential election campaigns is, in general, a constitutional exercise of federal power.[267] It also ruled that the elaborate disclosure and reporting requirements violate no right of speech, assembly, or privacy, except when an individual or organization can show that disclosure will result in the kind of focused and insistent intimidation, harassment or reprisal proved in *NAACP v. Alabama ex rel. Patterson.*[268] The majority also sought to chart a constitutional distinction between the ceilings upon expenditures, which were held to violate the first amendment, and the ceilings upon contributions, which were sustained. This is plainly the most difficult and important aspect of the case.

Counsel defending the expenditure ceilings had argued in various forms the basic point best expressed by Paul A. Freund: "[Those who make large expenditures for the mass media] are operating vicariously through the power of their purse, rather than through the power of their ideas, and . . . I would scale that relatively lower in the hierarchy of First Amendment values."[269] Conversely, the argument proceeded, the principal evil with which the Congress was concerned flowed from the nonspeech element, the money, and not as a consequence of the ideas expressed. The principles discussed earlier in this essay would lead from that predicate to the conclusion that, although some first amendment protection would extend to spending that supported speech, the expenditure regulation could be justified by showing that it served a substantial public interest.[270]

The Court held that political expenditures are protected by the first amendment as fully as speech itself:

---

rev'd in part, 424 U.S. 1 (1976). *See also* Leventhal, *Courts and Political Thickets*, 77 COLUM. L. REV. 345 (1977).

[267] Buckley v. Valeo, 424 U.S. 1 (1976).

[268] 357 U.S. 449 (1958).

[269] A. ROSENTHAL, FEDERAL REGULATION OF CAMPAIGN FINANCE 72–73 (1971) (commentary by Paul Freund).

[270] *See* pp. 47–48, 59–60 *supra*.

[T]his Court has never suggested that the dependence of a communication on the expenditure of money operates itself to introduce a nonspeech element or to reduce the exacting scrutiny required by the First Amendment.

. . . .

A restriction on the amount of money a person or group can spend on political communication during a campaign necessarily reduces the quantity of expression by restricting the number of issues discussed, the depth of their exploration, and the size of the audience reached.[271]

In the case of campaign contributions, on the other hand, ceilings were warranted because the danger of actual or apparent corrupt influence is markedly greater and there is little or no direct effect upon speech.

[A] limitation upon the amount that any one person or group may contribute to a candidate or political committee entails only a marginal restriction upon the contributor's ability to engage in free communication.

. . . .

. . . While contributions may result in political expression if spent by a candidate or an association to present views to the voters, the transformation of contributions into political debate involves speech by someone other than the contributor.[272]

Three Justices rejected the distinction between expenditures and contributions. The Chief Justice and Justice Blackmun judged both by the strict first amendment standard applicable to the regulation of pure speech, and therefore voted to hold all the ceilings unconstitutional.[273] Justice White saw both as regulations of the giving and spending of money, which were constitutionally justifiable because the nonspeech interests in public confidence in the integrity of government were suffi-

---

[271] Buckley v. Valeo, 424 U.S. 1, 16–19 (1976).

[272] *Id.* at 20–21.

[273] *Id.* at 235 (Burger, C.J., concurring in part and dissenting in part); *id.* at 290 (Blackmun, J., concurring in part and dissenting in part).

ciently urgent to justify the indirect effects upon first amendment interests in freedom of speech and association.[274]

A. Campaign Expenditures by Individuals and Political Committees

One important set of questions flowing from *Buckley v. Valeo* results from the uncertain scope of the ruling that the first amendment secures an individual the right to spend unlimited sums of money to advocate the election of the candidate of his choice, provided that his expenditures are not coordinated with those of the candidate. Although the challenge to the prohibition against expenditures in support of a clearly identified candidate was presented, the issue was discussed in the opinion only in general, abstract terms.[275] An individual may spend money to elect a candidate in a wide variety of ways. He may purchase radio or television time in which to deliver an address urging the candidate's election. He may incur expense in traveling around the country making speeches for his candidate. In these cases the individual is indeed speaking, and the expenditure is necessary to reach large numbers of people with his speech. Moving to the other extreme, the individual may take $100,000 to an advertising agency or a broadcasting station and pay whatever is necessary to rerun the candidate's most successful forty-five-second television spots. In such a case the spender says nothing, but supplies money that serves essentially the same function as a contribution. Although the general language of the opinion can be read to embrace both sorts of expenditure and every sort between the extremes, it can equally be read to deal only with expenditures made to reach more or larger audiences for one's personal expression.

In the context of a presidential campaign,[276] the issue has

---

[274] *Id.* at 257 (White, J., concurring in part and dissenting in part).

[275] 424 U.S. at 39–51.

[276] The problem is presently moot in the context of senatorial and congressional elections because Congress repealed the portions of the Act putting ceilings on total expenditures. Pub. L. No. 94-283, tit. II, § 201, 90 Stat. 496 (1976).

current importance. Both major party candidates in the 1980 presidential election were eligible for federal funding, which came to $29.4 million for each.[277] Each eligible candidate thereby committed himself and all political committees authorized by him to refrain from making expenditures or incurring obligations in excess of the $29.4 million limit.[278] Section 9012(f)(1) forbids any other "political committee . . . knowingly and willfully to incur expenditures to further the election of such candidate, . . . in an aggregate amount exceeding $1,000."[279] The restriction does not apply to individuals. Probably it does not apply to ad hoc informal groups. The evident intent is to limit all *organized* fundraising and campaign expenditures of the kind traditionally conducted by political parties and committees to the $29.4 million equal federal allowance.

On June 5, 1980, Senator Harrison Schmitt of New Mexico announced the formation of an "independent" committee intending to spend $20 to $30 million in support of the candidacy of Ronald Reagan. Its steering committee was made up of prominent and active Republicans such as Melvin Laird, George Romney, and William Miller. A separate group, made up of Nixon and Ford administration officials, announced that it aimed to spend up to $18 million on behalf of Mr. Reagan. The aggregate would have been greater than the total federal funding supplied each party under the assumption that no other campaign funds would be raised and spent, yet still other

---

[277] Federal Election Campaign Act of 1971, Pub. L. No. 92-225, 86 Stat. 3 (1972), *as amended by* Pub. L. No. 94-283, tit. I, § 112(2), 90 Stat. 486 (1976) (codified at 2 U.S.C. § 441a(b)(1)(B) (1976)), established a $20,000,000 ceiling on aggregate expenditures for presidential election campaigns, but provided as well that the limit would be raised in accordance with increases in the consumer price index as reported by the Secretary of Labor. 2 U.S.C. § 441a(c) (1976). The latest report pursuant to the Act showed an increase of 47.2% from the 1974 base period. 45 Fed. Reg. 8780 (1980). Thus the maximum allowable expenditures under the Act were $29,440,000 for each presidential candidate.

[278] In addition, there is a relatively small allowance for the expenditure of funds raised by the Republican and Democratic National Committees. *See* 2 U.S.C. § 441a(d)(3) (1976).

[279] I.R.C. § 9012(f)(1).

political committees were formed to solicit contributions and
make further expenditures. Common Cause and the Federal
Election Commission brought actions to enjoin the expenditures contemplated by the Schmitt group. A three-judge district court dismissed the complaints, but the decision will be
appealed to the Supreme Court.[280]

Section 9012(f) was not before the Court in *Buckley v.
Valeo*. The per curiam opinion in that case states,[281] and a
lower court subsequently ruled,[282] that the provisions binding
a candidate to expenditure ceilings upon voluntarily accepting
public funds do not violate the first amendment. That ruling
is scarcely determinative of whether the section 9012(f) restriction upon spending by "unauthorized," *i.e.*, independent, political committees is constitutional because the candidate cannot waive the independents' first amendment rights. On the
other hand, the invalidation of statutory expenditure ceilings
applicable to all elections can hardly be supposed conclusive
with respect to presidential election campaigns that the major
party candidates have agreed to conduct with federal funds.

Organized fundraising, purchase of television time, and
other political advertising by a political committee are clearly
types of conduct affecting speech and entitled to some degree
of first amendment protection. It can be argued, however, that
these activities are not speech itself, and therefore do not merit
the full shelter of the first amendment. The argument is given
point by asking whose right of speech is abridged by the
restriction. Those who give the money are not engaging in
communication. As in the case of a contribution directly to a
candidate, there is "only a marginal restriction upon the contributor's ability to engage in free communication" because
"the transformation of contributions into political debate involves speech by someone other than the contributor."[283]
Those who constitute the committee to raise and spend the

---

[280] Common Cause v. Schmitt, Civ. No. 80-1609 (D.D.C. Aug. 28, 1980) (order
issued denying injunction), *notice of appeal filed* (D.D.C. Sept. 26, 1980).

[281] 424 U.S. at 90–109 (upholding 26 U.S.C. §§ 9001–9012, 9031–9042 (Supp. IV
1974)).

[282] Republican Nat'l Comm. v. FEC, 487 F. Supp. 280 (S.D.N.Y. 1980).

[283] 424 U.S. at 20–21.

money do not engage in speech; their concern is to provide the money. Having combined contributions into a pool, the committee will simply turn it over to one or more advertising agencies to conduct an advertising campaign through the mass media. The space advertising will present the picture and slogans of the candidate. The television spots will present the visage and voice of the candidate taken from newscasts and previous television appearances. It would not be surprising to find an independent committee simply buying additional time to rerun the candidate's own spots. In short, the committee's activities are much more like the contributions held subject to regulation in *Buckley* than like the individual expenditures held immune. Furthermore, individual speech is in no sense involved because section 9012(f) applies only to the expenditures of an organized political committee.

This analysis might persuade the Court to limit or distinguish its earlier ruling with respect to the independent expenditures of individuals and informal groups, but the defenders of section 9012(f) will also need to deal with the portion of *Buckley v. Valeo* invalidating ceilings upon the aggregate expenditures of a candidate for Senator or Representative.[284] The raising and spending of money by an independent political committee differs from the raising and spending of money by a committee acting for the candidate in that the latter involves speech delivered or authorized by the candidate. An additional and perhaps more important difference is that Congress determined that section 9012(f)'s restriction upon organized fundraising and expenditures by so-called independent committees is a bulwark necessary to the success of public financing of presidential campaigns. Both the acceptability and the equity of conducting presidential election campaigns upon equal public funding of major party candidates depend upon eliminating other organized programs of large-scale fundraising and expenditure, which not only could seriously upset the balance but also would reintroduce many of the evils of private funding.

The ruling in *Buckley v. Valeo* that invalidated imposed

<hr>

[284] *Id.* at 54–59.

ceilings upon a candidate's aggregate expenditures rested partly upon the view that political spending is to be equated with pure speech, but also upon the opinion that so long as political campaigns are privately funded, the major evils associated with the growing role of money in political campaigns can be sufficiently alleviated by restricting the size of campaign contributions.[285] In the case of presidential campaigns, Congress turned away from private contributions. Accordingly, although the defense of the constitutionality of section 9012(f) would seem to require partial reexamination of views expressed in *Buckley v. Valeo*, it can accept the actual decision upon the issues presented to the Court.

B. Campaign Expenditures by Corporations and Labor Unions

First National Bank v. Bellotti[286] extended to corporations the first amendment right to spend money in political campaigns — at least in the context of a referendum. The First National Bank of Boston and other business concerns, desiring to spend corporate funds to defeat in a general referendum a proposed amendment to the Massachusetts Constitution authorizing a graduated individual income tax, sought a declaratory judgment invalidating as a violation of the first amendment a Massachusetts statute that prohibits any banking or business corporation from making any contribution or expenditure for the purpose of "influencing or affecting the vote on any question submitted to the voters, other than one materially affecting any . . . business or assets of the corporation."[287] The statute explicitly barred corporate expenditures made to influence any referendum upon the individual income tax.[288] The parties stipulated that experts were divided in opinion

---

[285] *Id.* "The major evil associated with rapidly increasing campaign expenditures is the danger of candidate dependence on large contributions. The interest in alleviating the corrupting influence of large contributions is served by the Act's contribution limitations and disclosure provisions rather than by § 608(c)'s campaign expenditure ceilings." *Id.* at 55.

[286] 435 U.S. 765 (1978).

[287] MASS. GEN. LAWS ANN. ch. 55, § 8 (West Supp. 1977).

[288] *Id.*

business corporations to make campaign contributions or expenditures flowed initially from the flagrantly corrupt practices of the 1880's and 1890's, the disclosures of the muckraking journalists, and the leadership of President Theodore Roosevelt.[302] In 1907, Congress made it a crime for any corporation to make a money contribution in connection with a federal election.[303] In 1943, the prohibition was made applicable to labor unions.[304] Later, the prohibition was extended to forbid "expenditures" as well as contributions, and to apply to primaries equally as to elections.[305] The prohibitions are now codified, as section 441b of the Federal Election Campaign Act.[306] More than half the states have essentially similar laws prohibiting the use of corporate funds to support political candidates.[307]

Rigidly logical extension of the reasoning in *Buckley* and *Bellotti* would lead to the conclusion that section 441b and similar state laws are unconstitutional. According to *Buckley*, independent individual expenditures, however large, are pure speech and give rise to too little danger of undue influence upon a candidate's conduct in office to justify restriction unless they are "controlled by or coordinated with" the candidate, in which case they would be treated as contributions. According to *Bellotti*, corporate expenditures are also speech, and speech cannot be curtailed because of the character of the "speaker," whether corporation or labor union. There is no reason to suppose that an "uncontrolled" and "uncoordinated" corporate expenditure of $25,000 or $50,000 to promote the election of a particular candidate will be either more or less corrupting

---

[302] *See* E. EPSTEIN, CORPORATIONS, CONTRIBUTIONS, AND POLITICAL CAMPAIGNS 10–12 (1968).

[303] Tillman Act of 1907, Pub. L. No. 59-36, 34 Stat. 864.

[304] War Labor Disputes Act, Pub. L. No. 78-89, 57 Stat. 167 (1943) (enacted for the duration of the war).

[305] Labor-Management Relations (Taft-Hartley) Act of 1947, § 304, Pub. L. No. 80-101, 61 Stat. 136 (current version at 2 U.S.C. § 441b (1976)).

[306] 2 U.S.C. § 441b (1976).

[307] *See, e.g.*, CONN. GEN. STAT. § 9-336b (1979); MASS. GEN. LAWS ANN. ch. 55, § 8 (West Supp. 1980); N.Y. ELEC. LAW § 14-116 (McKinney 1978); TEX. ELEC. CODE ANN. art. 14.06 (Vernon Supp. 1979).

than an expenditure of like size by the individual president of the same corporation. According to both opinions, the danger that individual ideas and voices will be drowned out by massive advertising campaigns is not sufficient to justify prohibiting vast expenditures for political advertising by individuals or corporations.

Predictions in this area are hazardous at best, but I think it unlikely that the Court will pursue the logic so rigidly as to hold section 441b unconstitutional. A footnote in the *Bellotti* opinion reserves judgment upon corporate expenditures in support of or in opposition to a candidate.[308] Justice Powell's dissenting opinion in *Pipefitters Local 562 v. United States*,[309] arguing that the predecessor of section 441b prohibits union contributions to a candidate made from the voluntary contributions of members to the union's political fund as well as from their dues, not only assumes the constitutionality of a prohibition but emphasizes the dangers to elective and legislative processes that would flow from "major participation in politics by the largest aggregations of economic power, the great unions and corporations."[310]

Although other distinctions are available, the argument in defense of section 441b will probably center upon the long history of legislative recognition of the corrupting influence of corporate and labor union money in politics. The danger is manifestly greater in an election than in a referendum, as Justice Powell observed in his footnote reserving judgment on section 441b,[311] because large expenditures to elect a specific

---

[308] 435 U.S. at 788 n.26.
[309] 407 U.S. 385 (1972).
[310] *Id*. at 443 (Powell, J., dissenting).
[311]

The overriding concern behind the enactment of statutes such as the Federal Corrupt Practices Act was the problem of corruption of elected representatives through creation of political debts. The importance of the government interest in preventing this occurrence has never been doubted. The case before us presents no comparable problem, and our consideration of a corporation's right to speak on issues of general public interest implies no comparable right in the quite different context of participation in a political campaign for election to public office. Congress might well be able to demonstrate the existence of a

candidate may create a corrupting obligation even though the spending is independently undertaken. If the Court is satisfied upon the last point, *Buckley v. Valeo*'s protection of political speech might be limited to expenditures by individuals and informal, unorganized groups, or even more narrowly to expenditures made by individuals and groups to enlarge the audience for personal expression.

Deciding whether the justification is adequate would seem to bring one back to the problem of separation of powers discussed in connection with the *Pharmacists* case.[312] To what extent should the judiciary substitute its judgment for that of the legislative branch upon the extent and seriousness of the danger that independent expenditures of corporations or labor unions will poison the political process and erode public confidence in government? Justice White's dissent in *Bellotti* criticizes the majority for substituting its judgment for that of the Massachusetts legislature "in the context of the political arena where the expertise of legislators is at its peak and that of judges is at its very lowest."[313] The observation seems partly justified, although Justice Powell relied partly upon the absence of evidence in the record or legislative findings.[314] In *Buckley v. Valeo*, the per curiam opinion implicitly withholds the deference to congressional findings for which Justice White contended in his *Buckley* dissent.[315]

First National Bank v. Bellotti marks an increase in liberty in the sense that the decision upholds a claim to freedom of

---

danger of real or apparent corruption in independent expenditures by corporations to influence candidate elections.

435 U.S. at 788 n.26 (citations omitted).

[312] *See* pp. 35–37 *supra*.

[313] 435 U.S. at 804 (White, J., dissenting).

[314]

If appellee's arguments were supported by [the] record or legislative findings . . . [they] would merit our consideration. But there has been no showing that the relative voice of corporations has been overwhelming or even significant in influencing referenda in Massachusetts, or that there has been any threat to the confidence of the citizenry in government.

435 U.S. at 788 n.26 (citations omitted).

[315] 424 U.S. at 259–66 (White, J., concurring in part and dissenting in part).

speech and sweeps aside a restriction imposed by government. Combined with the broadest reading of *Buckley v. Valeo*, however, it suggests two further consequences that seem almost certain to follow. First, the skill with which the charismatic candidate is packaged and sold would become more and more important, and ideas and reasons would become less and less effective. Second, the influence of organized groups would grow and the voice of the individual would diminish. If liberty means the opportunity of the individual man or woman to express himself or herself in a society in which ideas are judged principally by their merit, increasing the relative influence of organizations with large financial resources and shrinking the attention paid to truly individual voices means a net loss of human freedom.

VI. Conclusions

At the cost of overgeneralization, I venture a few concluding observations upon the Burger Court's decisions under the first amendment.

1. The expansion of first amendment guarantees against direct government interference with publication or with speakers in conventional public forums,[316] which took shape under Chief Justice Warren, has continued under Chief Justice Burger when the attempted interference is based upon the supposedly "harmful" tendencies of the message. The only notable exceptions lie in the area of pornography, hard and soft.[317] The only significant direct inhibition upon publication in the area of political reporting or debate is the limited liability for defamation of one who is not a public figure.[318]

The decade of the 1970's, however, brought many fewer initiatives than the two preceding decades. The major new departures were the extension of the first amendment to "com-

---

[316] *See* pp. 6–14, 20–32 *supra.*

[317] *See, e.g.*, FCC v. Pacifica Foundation, 438 U.S. 726 (1978); Young v. American Mini Theatres, Inc., 427 U.S. 50 (1976); Paris Adult Theatres I v. Slayton, 413 U.S. 49 (1973); Miller v. California, 413 U.S. 15 (1973).

[318] *See* pp. 14–19 *supra.*

mercial speech"[319] and the recognition of a first amendment right of both individuals and corporations to make at least some kinds of political expenditures in connection with referendums or election campaigns.[320] If the *Richmond Newspapers* decision is indeed the harbinger of a new first amendment right of access to governmental proceedings or information in the possession of the government, as Justice Stevens asserted in a concurring opinion,[321] it may come to outrank in importance all other first amendment decisions of the Burger Court.

2. The decisions of the 1970's do not substantially affect the doctrines limiting abuse of the state's power to regulate the time, place, and vehicle of communication because of interference with competing public interests unrelated to the content of the message. The most important developments in this area were probably (1) the extension of "speech" to include the use of crude, shocking, and perhaps even personally insulting epithets;[322] and (2) the establishment of a firm doctrinal principle invalidating otherwise justifiable regulations of time, place, or vehicle of expression when tied to the content of the message.[323] While some commentators credit the Burger Court with establishing a first amendment right of access to a public forum,[324] I find little support in the cases for that conclusion, not because the Court has rejected it but because the availability of a wide variety of public forums has made it unnecessary to put the proposition to a test.

3. The press has been notably unsuccessful in the effort to obtain special privileges or immunities from the duties normally incident to the administration of criminal justice and the conduct of litigation.[325]

4. The most striking aspect of the work of the Burger

---

[319] *See* pp. 32–38 *supra*.
[320] *See* pp. 68–74 *supra*.
[321] 100 S. Ct. at 2831 (Stevens, J., concurring); *see* pp. 25–28 *supra*.
[322] *See* pp. 49–52 *supra*.
[323] *See* pp. 52–56 *supra*.
[324] *See* pp. 56–59 & n.205 *supra*.
[325] *See* pp. 62–67 *supra*.

Court has been the insistence of the Justices upon presenting individual views, and their persistence in advancing those views even after a majority has disagreed. This is not a new development, but the trend has become more pronounced.

An outsider can only speculate about the explanation. Perhaps the fragmentation is just one more symptom of a highly individualistic, inward-looking period. Perhaps it results from the breaking down of an older body of law under the pressures of legal positivism and legal realism. It may also be the result of the increasing use of law clerks who write opinions to justify their Justices' votes. Because each Justice has a number of law clerks and typically none serves more than one or two years, a heroic effort by a Justice would be required to impart unity of philosophy and authorship to the law clerks' drafts.

Cases that reach the Supreme Court are usually complex. There is almost always something to be said on either side, and also for intermediate accommodations. Dissent is both inevitable and sometimes desirable. Diversity of opinion is also more creative than consensus. A single Justice's offbeat suggestion may catch hold and profoundly shape the law. But the Supreme Court has additional functions. A greater effort to obtain consensus, perhaps by shortening opinions and limiting them to points of common agreement, might beneficially reduce the volume of concurring and separate opinions.[326] Continuous fragmentation could well diminish not only the influence of the Court but the ideal of the rule of law.

5. The first amendment decisions of the 1970's seem to me to bear other marks of an exceedingly pragmatic and particularistic jurisprudence, even though doctrinal development is not always neglected. Quite likely, the wide variety of subjects of public discussion, and of public and private purposes served, is driving first amendment law beyond the old simple dichotomy between protected and unprotected speech, but if this differentiation is to occur, the categories should be artic-

---

[326] See The Supreme Court, 1979 Term, 94 HARV. L. REV. 75, pt. III (1980) (table 1). See generally Davis & Reynolds, Juridical Cripples: Plurality Opinions in the Supreme Court, 1974 DUKE L.J. 59; Note, The Precedential Value of Supreme Court Plurality Decisions, 80 COLUM. L. REV. 756 (1980).

ulately related to the philosophy underlying the first amendment. Similarly, the opinions often lack the full exposition necessary to fit the decisions into a coherent body of law. In other instances — for example, when confronted with actual or presumable legislative findings — different Justices, and sometimes the same Justices on different occasions, have proceeded upon inconsistent assumptions concerning the proper role of the judiciary in constitutional adjudication without addressing the recurring problem or acknowledging the apparent inconsistency.

6. The importance of these last two observations depends upon the importance attached to maintaining yet developing a coherent body of law. Both the value and the success of judicial review of constitutional questions seem to me to depend in the long run upon reducing so far as humanly possible the subjectivity of constitutional rulings and maintaining the distinction between the edicts of a council of wise men and the judgments of a court. In my view these purposes are best served by exercise of the American judges' traditional responsibility collectively to articulate their reasons for decisions in terms of the relevant body of ever-changing, ever-constant law.